Editor-in-Chief and Founder:
  Lyndon H. LaRouche, Jr.
Editorial Board: *Lyndon H. LaRouche, Jr. , Helga
  Zepp-LaRouche, Robert Ingraham, Tony
  Papert, Gerald Rose, Dennis Small, Jeffrey
  Steinberg, William Wertz*
Co-Editors: *Robert Ingraham, Tony Papert*
Managing Editor: *Nancy Spannaus*
Technology: *Marsha Freeman*
Books: *Katherine Notley*
Ebooks: *Richard Burden*
Graphics: *Alan Yue*
Photos: *Stuart Lewis*
Circulation Manager: *Stanley Ezrol*

INTELLIGENCE DIRECTORS
Counterintelligence: *Jeffrey Steinberg, Michele
  Steinberg*
Economics: *John Hoefle, Marcia Merry Baker,
  Paul Gallagher*
History: *Anton Chaitkin*
Ibero-America: *Dennis Small*
Russia and Eastern Europe: *Rachel Douglas*
United States: *Debra Freeman*

INTERNATIONAL BUREAUS
Bogotá: *Miriam Redondo*
Berlin: *Rainer Apel*
Copenhagen: *Tom Gillesberg*
Houston: *Harley Schlanger*
Lima: *Sara Madueño*
Melbourne: *Robert Barwick*
Mexico City: *Gerardo Castilleja Chávez*
New Delhi: *Ramtanu Maitra*
Paris: *Christine Bierre*
Stockholm: *Ulf Sandmark*
United Nations, N.Y.C.: *Leni Rubinstein*
Washington, D.C.: *William Jones*
Wiesbaden: *Göran Haglund*

ON THE WEB
e-mail: eirns@larouchepub.com
www.larouchepub.com
www.executiveintelligencereview.com
www.larouchepub.com/eiw
Webmaster: *John Sigerson*
Assistant Webmaster: *George Hollis*
Editor, Arabic-language edition: *Hussein Askary*

EIR (ISSN 0273-6314) *is published weekly
(50 issues), by EIR News Service, Inc.,
P.O. Box 17390, Washington, D.C. 20041-0390.
(703) 777-9451*

European Headquarters: E.I.R. GmbH, Postfach
Bahnstrasse 9a, D-65205, Wiesbaden, Germany
Tel: 49-611-73650
Homepage: http://www.eirna.com
e-mail: eirna@eirna.com
Director: Georg Neudecker

Montreal, Canada: 514-461-1557

Denmark: EIR - Danmark, Sankt Knuds Vej 11,
basement left, DK-1903 Frederiksberg, Denmark.
Tel.: +45 35 43 60 40, Fax: +45 35 43 87 57. e-mail:
eirdk@hotmail.com.

Mexico City: EIR, Sor Juana Inés de la Cruz 242-2
Col. Agricultura C.P. 11360
Delegación M. Hidalgo, México D.F.
Tel. (5525) 5318-2301
eirmexico@gmail.com

Canada Post Publication Sales Agreement
#40683579

Postmaster: Send all address changes to *EIR*, P.O.
Box 17390, Washington, D.C. 20041-0390.

Signed articles in *EIR* represent the views of the
authors, and not necessarily those of the Editorial
Board.

The End of an Epoch

EDITORIAL

War with China by Summer?

May 30—With Congress out of session until next week, and while Americans take time out to commemorate those who died in military service in past wars, some leading American and leading Chinese officials alike fear that war between the two nations is likely by Summer. The more astute know that if this is allowed to happen, it will quickly become a broader, multilateral nuclear exchange which will be, as a LaRouche PAC video put it, "Unsurvivable."

The most recent big step towards war was computer-nerd Defense Secretary Ashton Carter's long, highly-provocative May 27 commencement address to the U.S. Naval Academy. He told the cadets that he was going to focus his remarks on the Asia-Pacific, because it would define many of their future careers. He singled out the destroyer USS Lassen, which deliberately intruded in Chinese territorial waters last October, and he promised that we will "continue to fly, sail, and operate wherever international law allows." He accused China of "expansive and unprecedented actions in the South China Sea, pressing excessive maritime claims contrary to international law.... What's new and unique to this region is the assertion of claims, dredging, land reclamation, and militarization of features by several claimants but overwhelmingly by China.... China's cyber-actors have violated the spirit of the Internet—not to mention the law—to perpetrate large-scale intellectual property theft from American companies.

> Instead of working toward what [they call] 'win-win cooperation' that Beijing publicly says it wants, China sometimes plays by its own rules, undercutting those principles. A model like that

is out of step with where the region wants to go, and it's counterproductive—it's far from a 'win-win.' The result is that China's actions could erect a Great Wall of self-isolation, as countries across the region—allies, partners and the un-aligned—are voicing concerns publicly and privately, at the highest levels, in regional meetings, and global fora.

Carter went on to threaten China with superior U.S. weapons systems: the F-35 (which doesn't work), the P-8, "cutting-edge stealth destroyers," and numerous others.

> DoD maintains world-leading capabilities because we have made incomparable investments over decades,... It will take decades more for anyone to build the kind of military capability the United States possesses today. This strength is not simply about dollar figures—it's also about harnessing those dollars to a tremendous innovative and technological culture that only the United States has, and doing so to develop revolutionary technologies.

Carter's speech resembled a Hitler-style threatening rant, threatening war, and with about the truth-content of one of Hitler's tirades.

The Chinese have responded. *Global Times*, a newspaper owned by the Communist Party of China's *People's Daily*, published an unsigned editorial today which said, "U.S. Defense Secretary Ashton Carter Friday issued another sharp rebuke of China's actions in the South China Sea by warning Beijing that it is on a path to build a 'great wall of self-isolation.' He said the Pentagon's best weapons, including stealthy F-35 fighters, P-8 Poseidon maritime patrol aircraft, and the newest surface warfare ships, will be deployed to the Pacific theater...

The nature of Sino-U.S. relations will to a large extent determine the state of international relations in the Twenty-first Century. By pointing the finger at China with a bluffing posture, senior U.S. officials are eroding the foundation of peace in the Asia-Pacific. On the contrary, China has been stressing resolving disputes peacefully. Maintaining peace in the South China Sea is the common wish of all regional stakeholders....

Carter's words have been the most threatening China has heard since the end of the Cold War. They confirm some Chinese people's worries about the worst-case scenario in the Sino-U.S. relationship, in which Washington may translate its intention to counter China into real actions. The Pentagon may be willing to see confrontation between China and the United States. But the United States cannot overawe China by wielding a military stick. The People's Liberation Army can offset the U.S. advantage of equipment in the South China Sea with its size and proximity, and we are confident about countering the threat from the United States. Although a military contention will be harmful to China, we cannot retreat in the face of U.S. coercion. China must accelerate its pace to build modern defense capabilities. It should let the United States know that if it launches military attacks targeting China in the South China Sea, the United States will suffer unbearable consequences. China must enhance its ability to deter the United States and increase the U.S.' strategic risks of military threat against China. [emphasis added]

Now you too have joined the number of those who know this, and you have taken on, willy-nilly, the inescapable responsibility which accompanies that knowledge. Get it out everywhere for a start—but that's only the beginning. Ask yourself what Lyndon LaRouche would do.

EIRContents

www.larouchepub.com Volume 43, Number 23, June 3, 2016

Cover This Week

I. War and Empire

HELGA ZEPP-LAROUCHE TO LIVING MEMORIAL CONFERENCE

This Is the Crossroads for Mankind

This is an edited transcript of Helga Zepp-LaRouche's keynote address to the LaRouche PAC conference, "Living Memorial—Ending War and Terrorism," held in New York City on May 28 to observe Memorial Day in the United States. She addressed the conference via a live video connection.

Hello. Dear members of the LaRouche PAC, guests of the Schiller Institute, dear friends, it is a great pleasure for me to talk to you today. And as we are talking and thinking about the soldiers who have died in wars, I want to stress that in the time of thermonuclear weapons, it should be clear to anybody on this planet that war cannot be an option anymore to solve any conflict. Because if it were to come to the unthinkable, that you would have an exchange of nuclear weapons,— well, there are some theories right now, that you could have a limited nuclear war, a winnable, regional, nuclear war.

But I think that anybody who has studied the matter a little bit more in depth, as, for example, by reading the writings of Ted Postol, who has made the very elaborated argument as to why such a thing as a limited nuclear war does not and cannot exist,— Simply because, anybody who assumes that, overlooks the fundamental difference between conventional war, in which the aim is to defeat your enemy, to disarm him, and then to stop the war; and nuclear war, in which the

RTAmerica
Missile defense expert Ted Postol says that what the Obama Administration is doing creates a major national security risk.

LPAC TV
Helga Zepp-LaRouche addressing the "A Living Memorial: Ending War and Terrorism."

logic is that once it starts, all existing weapons will be used and they will be used instantly. And if it were to come to this point, it would mean the immediate extinction of civilization.

I think that was clearly understood at the height of the Cold War. You had the Mutually Assured Destruction (MAD) doctrine, in which it was very clear that either we survived together or we all die together. But that MAD strategy has been eroded for quite some time; because now you have all kinds of scenarios with the idea of winning war by having smarter, smaller, leaner, more usable, more precise, nuclear weapons and delivery systems, and that therefore you could use them. But that is now a mortal danger to civilization. We have been warning of that for quite some time. We made a video called *Unsurvivable*. We made many speeches about it, and we were almost—with few other people—

the voice of one calling in the desert. But now, in the last several weeks, there has been a sudden eruption of awareness on the part of many who are now speaking out, warning that things have gone completely haywire.

On the Edge of Nuclear War

This is all happening in the face of several acute strategic crises: one on the Russian border in Eastern Europe, another one in Southwest Asia, still another one over Korea, and another one over the South China Sea. Each one of these conflicts could become the trigger point for a global nuclear war. And people are really freaking out, because the upcoming NATO summit, which will take place at the beginning of July in Warsaw, is scheduled to manifest all kinds of changes, such as moving four major battalions of 1,000 troops each into the Baltic countries; of linking, at the time of that July summit, the recently installed ballistic missile defense component in Romania with the Aegis class destroyers already deployed in the Baltic Sea, the Black Sea, and elsewhere. And that buildup is reaching very quickly a point at which Russia has said that it cannot tolerate a continuous building of this ballistic missile system, because it's clearly aimed at Russia, and it's clearly aimed to take out the second-strike capability of Russia, and it has never been what was always the pretext, it has never been against the supposed missile threat from Iran.

Two or three years ago, the Russian military produced video animations showing that the systems installed now in Poland, in Romania, in Bulgaria, in Spain, and on these warships, are really assigned to hit Russia. But especially after the P5+1 deal with Iran, containing the danger of missiles coming from Iran, there is no more such pretext. Now it has been noted by people such as the New York University professor Stephen Cohen, that this buildup is very clearly with the intent to launch a war. Another very important spokesman in

www.RussianCenterNY.org
Stephen Cohen, Russian Studies and Politics professor at New York University and Princeton, has stated that the military NATO buildup in eastern Europe is being done to intentionally launch a war against Russia.

Russia, General Leonid Ivashov, has said that what we are seeing right now are clear steps in preparation for war.

It is very significant that even in Germany, Michael Stürmer, whom I would characterize as a staunch Atlanticist, someone belonging absolutely to the mainstream establishment, last week published a very important article in the conservative daily

Creative Commons
General Leonid Ivashov has said that what we are seeing right now are clear steps in preparation for war.

newspaper *Die Welt* with the headline, "No Protocol Will Save Us From Nuclear War." And there he talks about the modernization of nuclear weapons and the fact that there are supposedly fewer of them. Even so, one has to say that the Obama administration has eliminated fewer nuclear weapons from the stockpile than any earlier post-Cold War administration, and the rate of reduction has been slowing down significantly.

This Michael Stürmer notes that one should not assume that because these nuclear weapons become fewer and smaller, that this is good news. To the contrary, it is more reason to worry, because the very idea that these weapons are usable is lowering the threshold for them to actually be used. And then he says that during the Cold War, the military and political leadership had a very clear understanding of what Mutually Assured Destruction would mean, namely the annihilation of all of mankind. But now we have new

Michael Stürmer, chief correspondent for the conservative newspaper Die Welt, *headlined a recent article: No Protocol Will Save Us from Nuclear War.*

generations of both political and military leadership, which don't even pay attention to it anymore. And, he said, all of these almost fatal incidents, which are taking place now almost every day—either over the Baltic Sea, or in the Black Sea, or in the South China Sea—would have, in former times, set off the alarms at the highest possible level, because people recognized how quickly such an accidental almost-incident could lead to global war.

Other statements in recent months have made very clear that the systems of both NATO and Russia are kept in launch-on-warning status, and therefore the window for decision-making for either side—the President of the United States or the Russian President—is about 3 to 6 minutes, at best half an hour. So we are sitting on a potential Armageddon, which if people would just think about it, they would really do everything possible to stop it.

Right now there is a growing awareness of this. In a hearing in the U.S. Senate, Senator Dianne Feinstein commented on the United States now committing $1 trillion in the next decades to modernize its nuclear arsenal, including the tactical nuclear weapons, the B-61-12, which are stationed mostly in Europe. She noted that this makes the idea of using these weapons more within reach, and that alone is utterly immoral because of the implication that it could lead to the extinction of civilization.

We have a situation similar to that in Europe, right now, in the South China Sea. There is a lot of propaganda that China is supposedly aggressively taking land. Nothing could be further from the truth. All that China is doing, is putting installations on some of these islands which historically it has claims to, going back to the Ninth Century. And every other country in the region—the Philippines, Thailand, Vietnam—is doing the same thing, and has been doing so for a long time. Not one freighter has been prevented from traveling. So the whole argument that China is violating the freedom of navigation, which has been put forward by the United States, is simply not true. And all the incidents were caused by U.S. ships' violations of the 12-mile zone around these islands or by overflights, which are also a breach of international law.

A Question of Intention

So we are really at the edge. I must say I got a very, very eerie feeling when I received reports that Obama, before he went to Hiroshima, not only did *not* apologize for the U.S. having dropped nuclear bombs on Hiroshima and Nagasaki, for which there was, in reality, no reason. That attack did not save the lives of a million

Ukrainian Antifascist Solidarity

Ukrainian neo-Nazis after the coup display their symbol, the Wolfsangel, *used by divisions of the Waffen-SS in World War II. The symbols of the Nazi and white supremacist organizations in Ukraine have been protected by law since the Feb. 21, 2014 coup.*

American soldiers, as claimed by the official narrative of the Truman Administration. It was very well known that Japan had already negotiated, with Vatican mediation, a resolution and capitulation. So dropping the bombs on Hiroshima and Nagasaki was simply to establish the principle of *Schrecklichkeit* [horror], to demonstrate to the Soviet Union at that point the power of nuclear weapons.

So, Obama did not apologize, which is telling in itself. But in an interview with Japanese TV, when he was asked what he thought about the dropping of the bomb on Hiroshima, he said, "I have been President now for seven and a half years, and having been a wartime President myself, I can understand that presidents, under those conditions, could be forced to make such decisions." I think people better wake up to where we are really at.

We have no reason to go to war. Russia is not aggressive; don't believe it for one second. Every step

Russia has been taking, especially since beginning of the Ukraine crisis, has been for war avoidance. The Ukraine crisis began with the effort to pull Ukraine into the EU Association Agreement. That was unacceptable to President Yanukovich who, at the time, reacted strongly and fled from the EU Summit, because he realized that signing the agreement would have given NATO control over Ukraine. And it would have opened up the Russian market for all EU products, which was unacceptable for Russia. So he rejected the agreement.

Then the Maidan protests were sprung against the Ukrainian government. Then came the coup on February 21, 2014, a coup organized by Nazis; everyone knew that the organizers were going back to the Stepan Bandera tradition. So the West went along with that. It led to the terrible conditions inside east Ukraine, and as a reaction to all of this Russia annexed Crimea. It is wrong to say that Russia was aggressive in taking the Crimea, because Russia reacted at each single step as Russia reacted to the entire breaking of the promises which were given to Gorbachov, but also to other people at the time when the Soviet Union disintegrated, that NATO would not extend its troops to the border of Russia. Then you had the color revolution in Ukraine, the sanctions, all of this has been correctly characterized by Russia as being forms of a hybrid war which is already going on, with the ultimate aim of regime change in Moscow. Madeleine Albright and the former Green Party Foreign Minister of Germany, Joschka Fischer, said at one point that Russia has too much territory and too many raw materials; is it going to be allowed to exploit these raw materials all by itself?

War Avoidance

There is also the same kind of geopolitical intention for regime change against China, which I don't want to elaborate on now; we can possibly do so in the discussion. But what I'm saying is that neither Russia nor China is aggressive. Don't believe these media lies, which are forms of pre-war propaganda. As a matter of fact, the absolute opposite is true. China has initiated a policy which is a war avoidance policy; it is actually the only perspective for overcoming geopolitics which has been put on the table by anyone. In September 2013, when Xi Jinping announced in Kazakhstan the New Silk Road, this was a policy in the tradition of the ancient Silk Road which, 2000 years ago, during the Chinese Han administration, involved an exchange of

Former Chairman of the Joint Chiefs of Staff, Martin Dempsey, warned many times of the danger of the United States falling into the Thucydides trap.

goods, of culture, of ideas. It led to a tremendous increase in the prosperity of all the nations participating in the Silk Road at that time; and what China is now offering with the New Silk Road, is doing exactly the same thing.

This project, which is now almost three years old—in September it will be three years since it was started—already involves 70 countries; its impact has been mainly in Asia, along the ancient Silk Road, but it is also now reaching out to the ASEAN countries, to Iran, to Africa, to Egypt, to India. This is now a project which is pursuing a completely different principle. It is not the casino economy of the trans-Atlantic sector; it is the idea to build infrastructure, to have a banking system associated with it which is not investing in high-risk speculation, but providing the necessary credits to solve the incredible lack of infrastructure which has been the result of the policies of the IMF and the World Bank, which have deliberately denied developing countries access to credit for infrastructure.

The New Silk Road policy, and the banking system associated with it—the Asian Infrastructure Investment Bank, the BRICS New Development Bank, and the new Shanghai Cooperation Bank which was just started; also the Silk Road Fund, the Maritime Silk Road Fund, the SAARC Development Bank (the South Asian countries)—all of these banks represent a completely different model of banking and economic cooperation. And they have invited the United States to join. Xi Jinping has repeatedly said, this is an open concept for every country on the planet. We want to have a win-win perspective where, naturally, China has its advan-

8   End of an Epoch

EIR   June 3, 2016

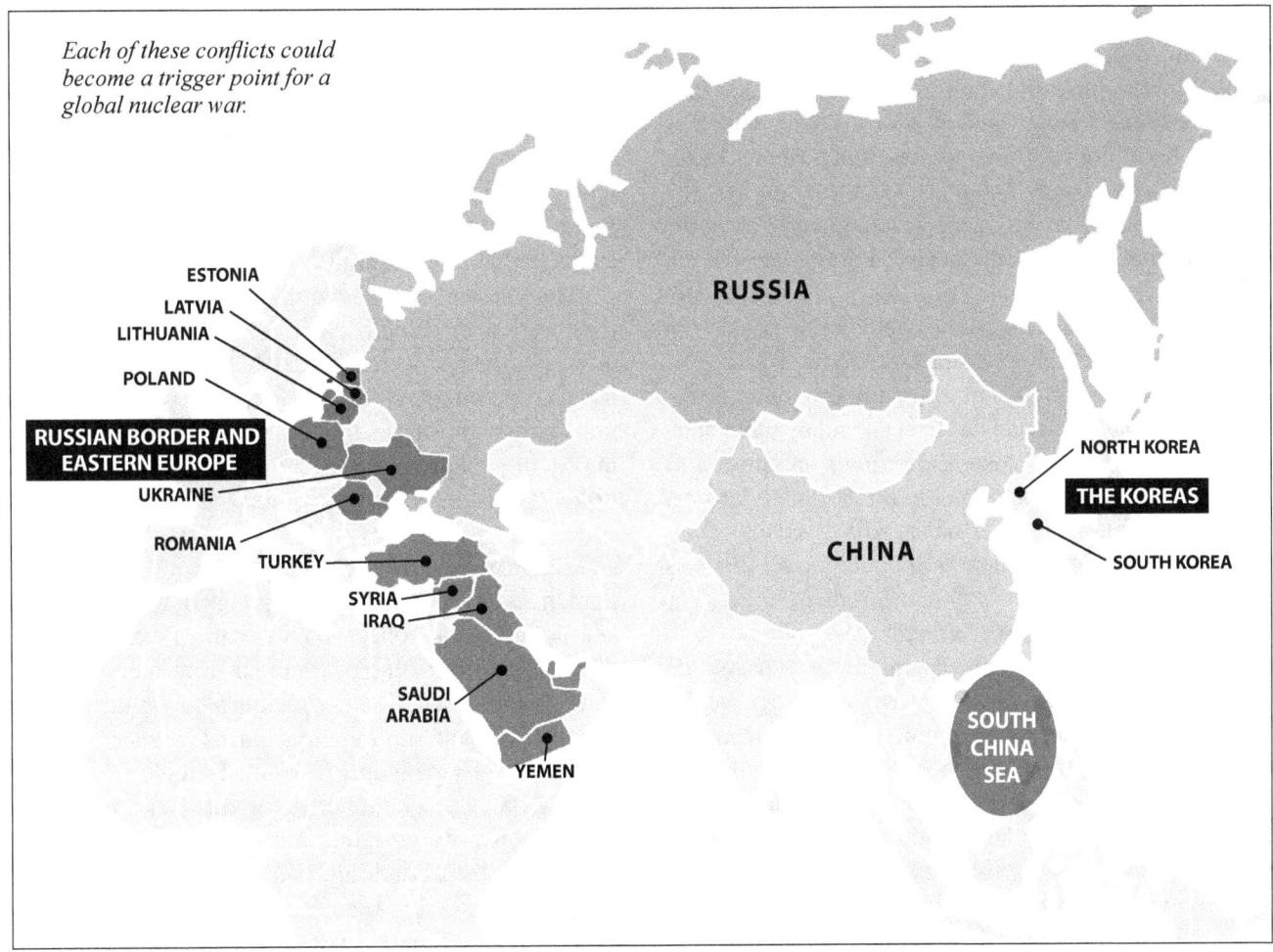

Each of these conflicts could become a trigger point for a global nuclear war.

ESTONIA
LATVIA
LITHUANIA
POLAND
RUSSIAN BORDER AND EASTERN EUROPE
UKRAINE
ROMANIA
TURKEY
SYRIA
IRAQ
SAUDI ARABIA
YEMEN
RUSSIA
NORTH KOREA
THE KOREAS
SOUTH KOREA
CHINA
SOUTH CHINA SEA

tages; but every other country has its own advantages if it participates.

The Problem Is the British Empire

Now, where does the war danger come from? Why are the United States, and the EU, and Great Britain,— why are they not simply joining? Well, the problem is the British Empire. The problem is that the United States, in reality, is run by the idea that there must be a unipolar world run on the basis of the special relationship between the British Empire and the United States. And unfortunately President Obama has completely bought into this idea, which is really a continuation of the neocon policy, presented by such people as Paul Wolfowitz and Richard Perle at the end of the 1990s. They called it the Project for a New American Century. And that is the idea, that, with the collapse of the Soviet Union, there is only one superpower left, and that superpower has the right, basically, to deploy militarily around the globe; that that superpower will not allow

any nation or group of nations to bypass the United States in terms of economic, political, or military power.

The problem for this outlook is that the unipolar world, in reality, does not exist anymore. Because China is rising; all of Asia is rising. China is already producing many more high technology goods for export than the United States. It is producing more scientists, more engineers. It is just much more future oriented, as you can see by the most fantastic space program that China has, while NASA has been dismantled. But not only is China rising, but many countries in Asia are rising. India, for example, India has the largest economic growth rate in the world, about 8%. Other countries are totally committed to being modern, middle class countries by 2020 or 2025, such as Malaysia; even Ethiopia wants to be very soon a normal, developed country. This is happening and you cannot stop that desire for development of all these nations around the globe.

The problem is that the trans-Atlantic sector is about to blow up financially. The G-7 meeting has just concluded. The G-7 is supposedly the group of the most important countries economically, or that's what they think they are. In reality, their influence is shrinking, so that even the German tabloid *Bild Zeitung*, which is read by 8 million people every day, had a banner headline saying that the G-7 summit was the summit of the seven dwarves. That was a correct characterization; the only reasonable person at that G-7 summit, was—a big surprise—Japanese Prime Minister Shinzo Abe. Because he went into the summit after coming back from a visit to Sochi, where he met extensively with President Putin and concluded many, many economic deals, gas and oil in the Russian Far East and many other such projects, which he did despite enormous pressure from the Obama Administration not to do. He came into the summit and said, "Look, we have to discuss the fact that the western financial system is about to have a crisis as big as 2008," the crisis of Lehman Brothers.

That fell on deaf ears. Obama said, no, no such thing, we are in an upswing. So the final communiqué of that summit said the upswing is continuing, we are all doing fine. Now nothing could be further from the truth. Because right now, the too-big-to-fail banks, if one of these banks were to go bust, the entire system could evaporate. You have right now the ridiculous debate around helicopter money. That is the idea that the last resort of the central banks is to print money electronically, the equivalent of throwing dollar bills out of helicopters over cities, to prevent a crash from happening, which was the crazy idea of Ben Bernanke many years ago, but they are now doing it.

The bankers have negative interest rates. They are issuing hundred-year bonds. If you want to make a donation to the bank, then buy a hundred-year bond, because it is an illusion. It will evaporate, and if you sell such a bond before the hundred-year term is up, you will lose a lot of money. So it is a complete swindle to get people who have savings to invest in the banking machine. The fact that people are buying these bonds, shows you that the confidence in the markets has really shrunk to an abysmal point.

Two Opposing Policies

This is the real war danger. Because there are people in the trans-Atlantic world who are absolutely determined not to allow Asia to rise, who are about to commit exactly the mistake that the former Chairman of the Joint Chiefs of Staff, General Martin Dempsey, warned of many times, to fall into the Thucydides trap, the trap described by the historian Thucydides. That was the conflict between Sparta and Athens in ancient Greece, in which the fear of each, over the rise of the other, led to the Peloponnesian War and the destruction of Greek civilization. Greece has never regained the importance it had at that time. Dempsey had warned that the United States should not make the same mistake; but that is exactly what is happening.

Many, many changes in the world are taking place right now with at high speed. As I said, Japan is, right now, swinging towards the BRICS coalition, the Silk Road coalition. Obviously, if Japan has very good relations now with Russia, that is a good stepping stone for improving relations with China as well. The Indian Prime Minister, Narendra Modi, was just in Iran and concluded, together with President Hassan Rouhani and the President of Afghanistan, Ashraf Ghani, long-term investments for the development of Chabahar Port and its industrial zone, which is part of extending the Silk Road from China to Iran and from there to India and to Afghanistan. [See "Breakthrough on the Gulf of Oman," by Tanu Maitra in this issue.]

The former Afghan President, Hamid Karzai, had already stated at a conference in New Delhi in March, that the only way Afghanistan can be pacified is by making it a hub of trade and commerce for the New Silk Road connection between Asia and Europe. The President of India, Pranab Mukherjee, was just in China for a four-day visit, and also concluded many, many deals. He made a beautiful speech referring to the long, ancient cultural collaboration and exchange between China and India. He said, "If our two nations," which are the biggest in the world in terms of population, together more than 2.5 billion people, "If our two countries work together, there is nothing we cannot accomplish on this Earth."

So, you have right now two completely different sets of policies. The trans-Atlantic world is in fear of losing its unipolar control and is preparing for war; however, people in Europe are freaking out about it. There is much discussion about ending the sanctions against Russia. The French National Assembly has voted to end the sanctions. Just yesterday, a commission of the French Senate also voted against sanctions. Italian Prime Minister Matteo Renzi is against sanctions, and he is going in June to the St. Petersburg economic summit, which is clearly not what the United States would like to see. In Germany, half (or even more) of the country is in favor of ending the sanctions.

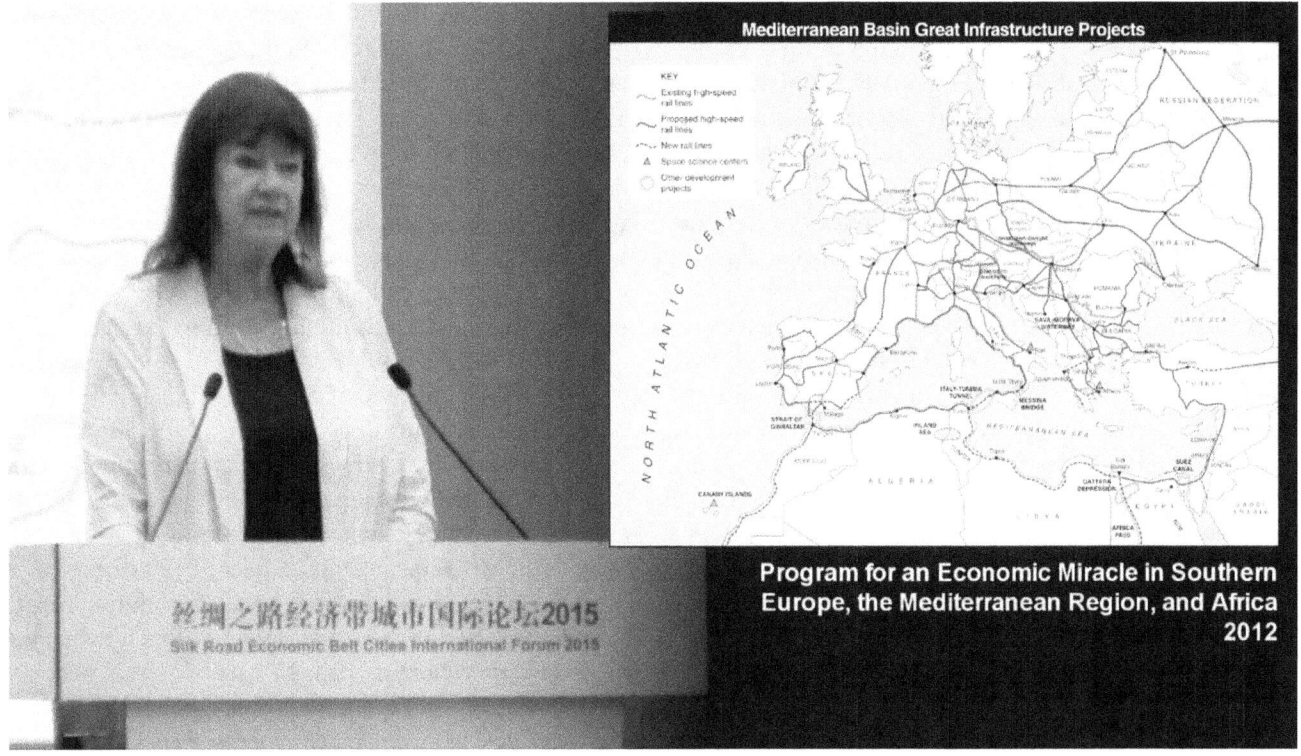

Program for an Economic Miracle in Southern Europe, the Mediterranean Region, and Africa 2012

Helga Zepp-LaRouche making a presentation on the alternative to geopolitical war and terrorism offered by the New Silk Road, at an International Forum on the New Silk Road in Yiwu, Zhejiang Province, China, June 18-19, 2015.

And right now, people realize they have to make a choice: Do they stay in the war machine in the trans-Atlantic world, or do they side with those countries which represent the future?

The Branching Point

We have right now a branching point in history. Do not think that this situation will last forever; it is changing very quickly. I think the decision as to which direction mankind will go, will be made in the coming weeks, in the month of June and not much beyond that. There is a war danger for this summer; people are talking about a danger of war with Russia in 2017. There is a book out by a neocon with that title. People are very worried that the crisis in the South China Sea may explode this summer, or be exploded. There comes a point of no return.

So, we have to really think of what can be a way out. But I must bring in one other problem. In Europe right now, we are in complete turmoil because of the influx of the largest number of refugees since the end of World War II. Last year about 2 million refugees came to Europe; this year it is expected to be a little less, because the EU is now committing a murderous policy by

using the military means of Frontex to drive the refugees back. Many of them are drowning in the Mediterranean. The EU is making extremely dirty deals with Turkey and Saudi Arabia to get their help in preventing the refugees from entering the EU.

It will not work; it already has led to the complete discrediting of the EU. No one from the EU should talk anymore about humanitarian values, or even human values, when the EU is carrying out such murderous policies against the refugees. But it should be obvious that you will not solve that problem by building new walls around every country; that is the end of the EU anyway. And also, not walls around the outer borders of the EU. But you need to eliminate the underlying cause that results in people risking their lives, with a 50% chance they might die in trying to get to Europe. They are running away from wars, hunger, and other catastrophes in Southwest Asia and in Africa. In the case of Southwest Asia and Libya, it's clearly the result of American and British wars, NATO wars all based on lies, which have led to a complete explosion there. And in the case of Africa, it's the result of nearly 50 years of induced increased death rates because of the conditionalities of the IMF.

Now there is a way out. As I said, China, India, and Iran are now all working to extend the Silk Road into Iran and Afghanistan; and the obvious idea is that we need a Marshall Plan-Silk Road approach towards the entire Southwest Asia region—from Afghanistan to the Mediterranean, from the Caucasus to the Persian Gulf. We have to have a real development strategy to conquer the desert in this region through the development of new sources of fresh water—peaceful nuclear energy for desalination of large amounts of ocean water; temporary use of aquifers where they are abundant; and ionization towers to precipitate the moisture in the atmosphere. We can do everything. These countries, which once home to blossoming cultures, can blossom again to give a future to the younger generations. And it is already on the way because the neighbors are committed to do that.

All we have to do is convince the United States and the European countries to participate in such a Silk Road-Marshall Plan for the Middle East and for Africa. It would be so easy to eliminate poverty; we could do that in half a year. No person would have to die of hunger anymore, because the technologies all exist; and if you then build infrastructure—ports, railway systems, waterways, highways, food processing. Build new cities, build advanced technologies in all countries of Africa and Southwest Asia. It could be turned around in a few years, and in one or two generations these regions could be as developed as the United States or Europe were in the 1970s. I'm not saying now, but as they were in the 1970s.

To Preserve the Human Identity

So, why don't we move in this direction? There is no good reason. We will lose identity as human if we don't do it. I think we have never faced such a challenge as right now. It is extremely important to remember that this planet is inhabited by only one human race, contrary to the poison of the new racists and the new fascists, unfortunately now on the rise. As in the 1930s, you have the rise of racism and fascism. It is old wine in new bottles; the contents of these bottles remains the same. Anyone who says the refugees or foreigners are genetically different, or have different reproduction schemes, and therefore must be kept out,— these are racists in new clothing. We must absolutely establish the idea that what makes us human is that every child born on this planet, is gifted with a potentially limitless potential to be a genius.

The fact that we don't have more geniuses on the planet right now is not due to the nature of the human being, but to the conditions of life that so far have not allowed the best development of every child born. If all children benefited from education, a decent living standard, and a culture of vision and hope for the future, we would have an increase of geniuses in the world. That would really show that mankind is in the infancy stage, maybe even the embryonic stage of its development.

If you want to evade the fate of the dinosaurs—that is, if you don't want to vanish—you have to make that evolutionary jump, so that we are no longer defined by blood and soil, or territory, or color of our skin or hair. We are defined, rather, by that which is common to all of humanity, that we can all be beautiful souls. That we can not only develop limitless new insights into the laws of the Universe and make scientific discoveries of physical principles leading to tremendous breakthroughs in science and technology, but that we can also become better human beings. That we can become more beautiful in our character, that we can become more loving; that we can become more artistically brilliant, that we can compose music at least as good as the great Classical music and beyond.

So I think we are really at a branching point, and you people there in New York have a very, very special responsibility. Because as Lyn has said, New York is a very, very special place in the United States; it is the birthplace of the United States. It's the place from which Alexander Hamilton operated. But even today, New Yorkers are generally more cosmopolitan, they are less chauvinist, they are more intelligent, they are more political. If we want to get the United States back to being a republic, a country which other countries wish to be allied with and not shrinking from it in fear and terror, then it is you, the New Yorkers, and your example shining out to the entire United States of America, which will turn this country around. So on this Memorial Day weekend, we have a tremendous moment. Think about the people who died in previous wars: We must have a solemn commitment that war should never become a means of resolving conflict. We must mobilize people around that idea, and the idea that humanity is really at the point of either finishing itself off, or of making an evolutionary jump—a jump by which we all define ourselves by the global development partnership in which we engage and the responsibility for building the bridge to a better age for future generations. I think we can do it.

The Anglo-Saudi Terror Machine Behind 9/11 Stands Fully Exposed

by Jeffrey Steinberg

May 26—Lyndon LaRouche issued a statement today that should resonate in Manhattan, on Capitol Hill, and around the world. He presented the essential truth about the Sept. 11, 2001 attacks on the World Trade Center and the Pentagon, at a moment when global attention has been finally directed at the actual criminals behind the worst terrorist attack on U.S. soil in history:

"A total injustice has been perpetuated from the beginning until now. The person who created the injustice has no right to contest anything now. The case is clear," LaRouche declared.

The point is that the Saudis and the British both committed a major crime against the citizens of the United States. When a nation's people has been betrayed by their own government on an issue built into the Constitution, an issue of Constitutional rights, such an issue is itself inherently a crime. The people of the nation have suffered a manifest crime against them. There's no basis for any support for what these criminals did; they don't have any standing. They're claiming that they have a standing within the injury that they created.

LaRouche was referring to the efforts by paid representatives of the Saudi Royal Family to continue to block the full release of evidence of their involvement in the 9/11 attacks. Over the past weeks, as pressure has mounted for the release of the 28 page chapter from the original Joint Congressional Inquiry into 9/11, and for passage of a clean JASTA (Justice Against Sponsors of Terrorism Act) bill, which would reinstate the Saudi Monarchy as defendants in a long-standing law suit by survivors and family members of the victims of the Sept. 11, 2001 attacks, the Saudis have unleashed a flood of cash and an army of lobbyists to spread disinformation and kill the efforts at achieving some measure of justice 15 years after the attacks that killed 2,977 innocent people.

Their efforts, aimed at protecting both the Saudi and British Monarchies from the full weight of prosecution for their role in the 9/11 massacre, however, have met with significant backlash—even among a small number of Members of Congress who have at long last started to ask the right questions and draw the appropriate conclusions.

An Exceptional Hearing

On May 24, a House Foreign Affairs Subcommittee, chaired by Rep. Ted Poe (R-Tex.), convened a hearing on the role of Saudi Arabia in the 9/11 attacks and other

Those giving testimony at the May 24 House Foreign Affairs subcommittee hearing included (left to right): Tim Roemer, Simon Henderson, Karen Elliot House, and Daniel L. Byman.

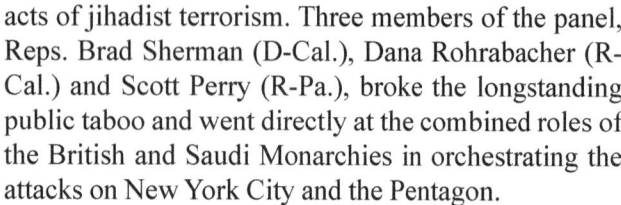

Rep. Dana Rohrabacher

Rep. Brad Sherman

acts of jihadist terrorism. Three members of the panel, Reps. Brad Sherman (D-Cal.), Dana Rohrabacher (R-Cal.) and Scott Perry (R-Pa.), broke the longstanding public taboo and went directly at the combined roles of the British and Saudi Monarchies in orchestrating the attacks on New York City and the Pentagon.

In a tense question and answer exchange with witness Karen Elliot House, Rep. Perry pressed for an explanation for why the United States was not doing more to force the Saudis to abandon their support for terrorism, through their bankrolling of Wahhabi schools and mosques around the world that have become breeding grounds for terrorist indoctrination and recruitment. House noted that when the original Saudi King wanted to invade and conquer Iraq, the British opposed the move, and the King ultimately had to go to war with some of his own supporters to fulfill the British demands. House admitted that the United States could certainly exert such pressure on the Saudis, but did not.

The mere mention of the historic British control over the Saudis in a public hearing on Capitol Hill was dramatic.

While *Executive Intelligence Review* has been in the forefront of documenting the Anglo-Saudi jihad machine, dating back to the scores of exposés of the role of "Londonistan" as the hub of world terrorism, where terrorists of all stripes have been given immunity and financial backing under the direct protection of the British Crown, the Anglo-Saudi relationship has been otherwise covered up and protected by a "bodyguard of lies."

Former Sen. Bob Graham, who chaired the original Joint Inquiry and has been a driving force behind the exposé of the Saudi Monarchy's hand in 9/11, had to resort to a fictional account of the Sept. 11, 2001 at-

tacks, in order to fully spell out the London-Riyadh connection, which he did spell out accurately in his novel, *Keys to the Kingdom*.

Al-Yamamah Revisited

At the heart of the modern British Crown control over the Saudi Wahhabi terror apparatus is the Al-Yamamah deal, which was personally negotiated in 1985 between Margaret Thatcher and Prince Bandar bin-Sultan, the son of the late Saudi Minister of Defense, who was for more than 20 years the Saudi Ambassador in Washington. Bandar and Thatcher used the cover of an oil-for-weapons barter deal to build up a string of offshore black funds that bankrolled the rise of Al-Qaeda, dating back to the final years of the Afghanistan War against the Soviet Union, and funded wars and coups all over the Third World for more than 30 years.

When the *Guardian* newspaper broke a corruption and kickback scandal around the Al-Yamamah deal in 2007, the British Serious Fraud Office opened an inquiry. The moment that the inquiry began to touch on the offshore secret accounts (in the initial instance, the Swiss accounts of Wafic Said, a top Al-Yamamah money launderer) at the real heart of Al-Yamamah, then-Prime Minister Tony Blair shut down the SFO investigation, invoking British national security.

In his own authorized biography, *The Prince*, Bandar boasted that the British and Saudi Monarchies had a special relationship, based on the ability of the two royal families to operate with absolute impunity—above the law.

Bandar's "finders fee" for the creation of the Anglo-Saudi Al-Yamamah terror program was at minimum $2 billion. At the time that Bandar and his wife Princess

Haifa were pouring money into the accounts of the Saudi intelligence officers working with the first two 9/11 terrorists to arrive in the United States, Al-Yamamah payoffs were being wired into their personal account at Riggs National Bank in Washington, originating in British Ministry of Defence accounts at the Bank of England.

The Saudi Royals Knew in Advance

Returning to the May 24 House hearings, Rohrabacher issued an impassioned opening statement, in which he asked: How many have to die before the truth about 9/11 comes out? This hearing, he declared, "is long overdue," and we must stop intentionally ignoring who financed the attacks. It is clear, he declared, "that the Saudi Royals were up to their eyeballs," warning that we will not recover from the consequences of 9/11 "unless we let the American people know."

At one point, after four witnesses delivered their opening statements, Rohrabacher resumed his attacks. He reported that four months before the 9/11 attacks took place, he had received information personally from a top Taliban official whom he had known from the time of the Afghan mujahideen war against the Soviet Army, that a major attack on U.S. soil was coming. Rohrabacher told the hearing participants that he had passed that information along to the relevant Executive Branch agencies and later to the Joint Inquiry and 9/11 Commission staffs.

He then polled the panel of witnesses, asking them if they believed that the Saudi Royal Family had to have had advance knowledge of the pending 9/11 attacks. Two of the four witnesses, former Congressman, Ambassador and 9/11 Commissioner Tim Roemer (D-Ind.) and Saudi expert Simon Henderson both raised their hands (panelists Karen Elliot House and Daniel Byman did not).

Both Sherman and Rohrabacher pounded the witnesses about the Saudi sponsorship of madrasas and so-called charities that spread Wahhabism around the globe, in almost all instances, creating the recruitment pool for jihadist terrorist groups. At one point, Rohrabacher told the hearing that one estimate is that the

Former FBI Director Robert Mueller

Former FBI Director Louis Freeh

Saudis have spent tens or hundreds of billions of dollars spreading Wahhabism around the world. Sherman added that it is "time to come clean." You cannot say that "the Saudis don't support terrorism."

The FBI Protection Racket

In early May, Rep. Sherman, in an interview with *The Hill,* had also blasted the Federal Bureau of Investigation for playing a pivotal role in covering up the crimes of the Saudis. Sherman cited an incident in 2011, when FBI agents detained former Sen. Bob Graham and his wife at Dulles International Airport and warned him to back off from his investigation into 9/11.

Sherman was furious at the action, telling *The Hill* that the FBI "took a former senator, a former governor, grabbed him in an airport, hustled him into a room with armed force to try to intimidate him into taking different positions on issues of public policy and important national policy, and the fact that he wasn't intimidated because he was calm doesn't show that they weren't trying to intimidate him."

The FBI protection of the Anglo-Saudi terror machinery has been a constant, long before the incident with Sen. Graham and his wife. In Sarasota, Fla., the FBI withheld over 80,000 pages of vital evidence about a prominent Saudi businessman with strong ties to the Royal Family, who hosted three of the 9/11 hijackers, including ringleader Mohammed Atta, at his residence in a gated community.

In the case of the Prince Bandar-funded hijackers in San Diego, Cal., for months they lived in the home of an FBI informant. That information, too was suppressed by top FBI officials, including then-Director Robert Mueller. Mueller's predecessor, Louis Freeh, retired from the Bureau and was hired to represent Prince Bandar—in the U.S. and British investigations into the Al-Yamamah deal.

The Saudi-British master criminals must be punished, but, more important, deprived of the power to ever again commit such atrocities. The U.S. government officials who have covered up for them must be purged and placed on trial.

The AfD Party: Old Wine In New Bottles?

PART TWO

by Helga Zepp-LaRouche, chairman of the German political party
Civil Rights Movement Solidarity, *BüSo*

The first article in this series appeared in the May 20, 2016 issue of EIR.

May 27—Horst Seehofer's claim that Angela Merkel's wrong immigration policy explains the rapid growth of the *Alternative für Deutschland* (Alternative for Germany party) is utterly oversimplified, and therefore wrong. Of course, the increase in the numbers of refugees was just what some politicians were waiting for, such as AfD "leader" Björn Höcke who roused the social anxiety of the population with demagogic arguments. Obviously refugees have never paid into health insurance funds or social security before, as one of the AfD's favorite mantras goes, but how could they have? Should they have gone to the American or British embassy in their countries some years ago, to take out a credit as restitution for the future destruction of their homes in geopolitically motivated wars?

This example makes clear that one can take a statement which, viewed narrowly, are not false *per se*—namely, "the refugees have never paid anything into the social security system"—and convey a falsehood with it, because it reduces a complex situation, such as why the refugees became refugees in the first place, down to a very narrow aspect of the issue. The first impulse behind Mrs. Merkel's refugee policy—when she said "We can do it!"—was correct, and in accordance with the Geneva Convention on refugees. Where she ultimately went wrong was that, while she said time and again that you must eliminate the causes of the refugee crisis, she never stated what these causes were.

To do that, one would have to address the role of Saudi Arabia in the September 11, 2001 attacks, as well as the wars based on lies that the U.S. waged in Southwest Asia in ostensible retaliation for those attacks, and the role of the "allies," Saudi Arabia and

CC/Olaf Kosinsky
Björn Höcke in the Thuringian Parliament, on Feb. 25, 2016.

Anti-islamic Pegida demonstration on Jan. 12, 2015 in Dresden, after the Charlie Hebdo shootings in Paris.

Turkey, in the financing of various Wahhabi-Islamist organizations from al-Qaeda to al-Nusra and ISIS, rather than relying on those two countries to stem the flow refugees.

In light of the uproar now raging in the United States over the well documented role of Saudi Arabia in support of terrorist organizations—the unanimous approval of the U.S. Senate for the Justice Against Sponsors of Terrorism (JASTA) law and the fight for the declassification of the famous, still secret 28 pages from the Congressional Inquiry on 9/11 come to mind—it is telling that Mrs. Merkel remains silent about the scandal of the Saudi role. Because the actual "causes of the refugee crisis" lie in this entire complex of events.

The second mistake that Mrs. Merkel is making is refusing to put on the table, together with Russia and China, a workable perspective for reconstruction of the liberated regions—initially Syria, and then the whole of Southwest Asia—which is only realizable in the greater framework of the New Silk Road.

According to the United Nations, there are already 60 million refugees or displaced persons worldwide. The head of the World Economic Forum, Klaus Schwab, recently said in Davos that, in the event of a further decline in the price of raw materials, one billion people from the Southern countries might make the trek toward the North. Should an uncontrolled collapse of the trans-Atlantic financial system occur—which is a real possibility given the negative interest rates of the central banks and the debate over helicopter money—this number could rise even higher due to the global impact.

Therefore the European Union's measures, which Mrs. Merkel went along with—to protect the outer borders of the European Union with the help of the Frontex organization and negotiate a horse-trade with Turkish President Erdogan—are not only totally unworkable, but they deny the refugees the protection they are due by international law. These measures expose that the "European values" which the EU constantly touts, have long since been transformed into barbarism. That is how the rest of the world sees it. The reality is that the whole world notices and discusses the wretchedness of the European Union on this question.

To emphatically repeat the point: The only way that we can remedy the greatest humanitarian catastrophe since the Second World War, is through comprehensive economic development—a New Silk Road Marshall Plan, if you will—for the entire Middle East and Africa, which builds up these destroyed, as well as entirely undeveloped countries, and provides a perspective for a better future to the people who live there. To do that, we must end the confrontation with Russia and China, and work together with Russia, China, India, Iran, Egypt, and many other countries for such a development perspective. The framework for this is already in place with China's New Silk Road and the offer for win-win cooperation.

It is precisely this unique perspective for a solution which the AfD rules out, because of its—to put it mildly—chauvinistic ideology. Above all, its attachment to neoliberal monetarist dogma makes it totally incapable of seeking solutions, much less of finding them.

The Conservative Revolution

The very idea that the AfD emerged as a reaction to the Euro crisis, the refugee crisis, or "political Islam" is completely erroneous. The Conservative Revolution, the tradition that the New Right explicitly espouses, and whose texts Götz Kubitschek's publication *Antaia* publishes, has existed in unbroken continuity since its emergence as a reaction to the "Ideas of 1789,"—thus for around 225 years, in manifestations which have in the best case only changed in appearance.

Among the extensive writings on the subject is Armin Mohler's slightly edited dissertation of 1949, published for the first time as a book in 1950 under the title, *The Conservative Revolution*. It aroused a storm of outrage at the time, because it was an attempt, only four years after the end of the Second World War, to treat fascist ideas quasi-academically, as if they had not directly caused catastrophic results for Germany and the world. Mohler explained in his book that the "Conservative Revolution" is a synonym for what is commonly identified as fascist.

The masterminds, according to Mohler, are small,

intellectually lively circles, highly explosive sects, loose combinations of the elite that remain in the background. They work out the programs "from above," which then are presented in simple words to the masses, who see themselves as getting a raw deal. Mohler described the relationship between the intellectuals and the common people in the following manner:

> The great party holds its masses together through organizational attachment to a doctrine adapted to the average person and narrowed down to catchwords, and only offers a place to superior minds to the extent that they take part in *taming the masses* and restrict their mental capabilities to the *esoteric realm*. But the majority of the above-average intellects gather in small circles, which resonate in constant mental tension, believe themselves to be the only ones with the true knowledge, and accuse the mass party of *Realpolitik*, betrayal of the "idea." [Emphasis added.][1]

Many leading members of the AfD see the Institute for State Policy (*Institut für Staatspolitik*), the think tank of the New Right which Götz Kubitschek and Karlheinz Weissmann founded in 2000, as the kind of place where such circles "resonate in constant mental tension." Training courses are regularly held there, which have been taken by 5,000 people. Björn Höcke refers to this institute as his "spiritual manna."

An Updated National Socialism

The *Frankfurter Allgemeine Zeitung* cited an e-mail that Bernd Lucke, who was recently thrown out of the AfD, wrote to the party's executive committee at the time Kubitschek and his wife Ellen Kositza sought to enroll as members. Kubitschek had turned up at Pegida and Legida events[2] in a black shirt and brown jacket, he wrote. "Whoever does not see in this a deliberate allusion to the fascist movements of Europe in the 1920s and 30s is a fool." At that time both were denied mem-

1. See "The Historical Roots of Green Fascism," by Helga Zepp-LaRouche, an article in two parts in *EIR*, April 13 and 20, 2007.
2. Pegida (Patriotic Europeans Against Islamization of the West) and Legida (Leipzig Europeans Against Islamization of the West) are anti-Muslim movements which have held mass demonstrations against immigration from Southwest Asia, especially in eastern Germany.

CC/Adam Fagen

Harvard biologist Edward O. Wilson speaking in Washington, D.C. in 2010.

bership. Today, Lucke is out, and Kubitschek is regarded by many AfD members as the intellectual leadership.

At the end of last year, Höcke delivered a striking lecture at the institute in which he presented, with astounding candor, the radical biological determinism typical of the New Right. He said that Mrs. Merkel's crazed asylum policy had set off a "self-feeding maelstrom" and that we must defend ourselves against asylum seekers, because Africa produces an "excess population" of 30 million people per year. Limits must be set by denying asylum, so that Africa can arrive at an ecologically sustainable rate of population growth.

According to Höcke, the problem is that Africa and Europe have two different reproduction strategies. Africa has the life-affirming mode of reproduction, referred to with a "small r," while Europe has a negative strategy for simple population replacement, referred to with a "large K." They therefore have two entirely different strategies for reproduction, which are now colliding over the optimal use of *Lebensraum.* (living space).

Seventy-one years after the end of the rule of National Socialism, it is inconceivable that anyone would dare to evoke the "excess population" of a certain population group, and *Lebensraum*. And subjecting people's demographic development to "ecologically sustainable" levels is exactly the same inhumane attitude that characterizes the eco-fascism of the green movement.

Höcke apparently borrowed the terms "small r" and "large K" from the American ecologists Robert MacArthur and Edward O. Wilson and their theories of the colonization of habitats.[3] The mode of thinking emerging here is worse than racism; it denies a large part of the human race its actual humanity, the quality which separates human beings as a creative species from all other forms of life, given their ability to exercise creative reason.

German citizens who are worried about the erosion of our society, about the security of our country, their own personal futures, and much else, should by no means make the mistake of falling for the "doctrine reduced to catchphrases." For hidden behind the phrases is an image of man that is incompatible with European or German values (if one understands these to include the humanism of Nicholas of Cusa, Wilhelm Leibniz, Felix Mendelssohn, Friedrich Schiller, and Albert Einstein), but instead is consistent with the racism which once threw our country into catastrophe. *To be continued.*

This article has been translated from German.

---

3. Ecologists Robert H. MacArthur and Edmund O. Wilson developed a theory of ecosystem stability in the 1950s, in which they posited two kinds of approaches populations could take for their survival. The "K" strategy was adopted by nations considered at or near their "carrying capacity," considered to be the maximum population that can be sustained by an environment; the "r" strategy characterizes nations which seek to expand their populations according to their biotic potential. MacArthur died in 1972, but Wilson continues to be a highly influential academic advocate of "sociobiology," a field that emphasizes the genetic determinism of human behavior (as also that of ant behavior, ants being the species on which he has done his academic study), and proposes policies based on those allegedly genetic differences.

Every Day Counts In Today's Showdown To Save Civilization

NEW REDUCED PRICE!

That's why you need EIR's **Daily Alert Service**, a strategic overview compiled with the input of Lyndon LaRouche, and delivered to your email 5 days a week.

For example: On Jan. 7, EIR's Daily Alert featured the British hand behind the pattern of global provocations toward war. Of special note is British Intelligence's role in instigating the Saudi Kingdom's attempt to set off a Sunni-Shia war. This religious war has been the intent of British strategy since the Blair-Bush attack on Iraq in 2003.

We also uniquely update you regularly on the progress toward the release of the suppressed 28 pages of the Congressional Inquiry on 9/11, which would expose the Saudi role.

Every edition highlights the reality of the impending financial crash/bail-in policies that would realize the British goal of mass depopulation.

This is intelligence you need to act on, if we are going to survive as a nation and a species. Can you really afford to be without it?

THURSDAY, JANUARY 7, 2016

Volume 2, Number 97

EIR Daily Alert Service

P.O. Box 17390, Washington, DC 20041-0390

- British Crown Pushing War and Genocide in 2016
- Financial Mudslide Goes On; Monetarist Tyranny Gloats over Bail-Ins
- Moody's Downgrades Portugal's Novo Banco
- Puerto Rico's Default: It's Every Vulture for Himself
- Wide Glass-Steagall Debate Set Off Again by Sanders Speech
- MI6 Mouthpiece Evans-Pritchard Touts Persian Gulf Chaos
- North Korea Tests a Miniaturized Hydrogen Bomb
- Uighur Terrorists Found in Indonesia
- Foreign Investors Are Flocking In to China

EDITORIAL

British Crown Pushing War and Genocide in 2016

SUBSCRIBE (e-mail address must be provided.)

EIR DAILY ALERT SERVICE

- ☐ **$100** one month (introductory)
- ☐ **$600** six months
- ☐ **$1,200** one year (includes EIR Online)

For mobile users, EIR Daily Alert Service is available in html

Name _____

Company _____

Address _____

City _____ State _____ Zip _____ Country _____

Phone (_____) _____

E-mail _____

I enclose $ _____ check or money order

Make checks payable to
EIR News Service Inc.
P.O. Box 17390, Washington, D.C. 20041-0390

Please charge my ☐ MasterCard ☐ Visa ☐ Discover ☐ Am Ex

Card Number _____

Signature _____

Expiration Date _____

EIR can be reached at:
www.larouchepub.com/eiw
e-mail: **fulfillment@larouchepub.com**
Call **1-800-278-3135** (toll-free)

II. The Grand Design

CREATIVITY AND PROGRESS

An Exchange between Xi Jinping And Lyndon LaRouche

by William Jones

May 29—A lengthy speech given earlier this year by Chinese President Xi Jinping was reprinted in the government paper, *Peoples Daily* on May 5. When economist and statesman Lyndon LaRouche was briefed on its contents, he made a direct and pointed response on the issue of creativity.

The *People's Daily* article had only been superficially covered in the Western media, which seemed to fixate on President Xi's comments that China's call for "supply-side" reform had nothing in common with what was designated by that term in the U.S. economic debate during the 1980s. But the speech had much more profound implications, which our Western media totally failed to notice. The speech was a lengthy elaboration by the Chinese President directed in particular to the cadre of the Chinese Communist Party, concerning the situation facing China today, a situation, as he pointed out, that is without precedent in the history of that nation. He also indicated that the "reform and opening up" policy initiated by Deng Xiaoping, which has allowed China to again take its place as a major economic power in the world, is itself at a new and untested stage of development. President Xi also indicated that the way forward will be arduous and filled with difficulties.

He gave a broad historical overview of the development of China during the last four decades, commenting briefly on the disastrous "leftist" shift in the 1960s, which led to the Cultural Revolution, that "10-year calamity" as he called it, which

set the economy back many years from the progress that had been made since the founding of the Peoples Republic in 1949.

With the "reform and opening up," China had achieved enormous success in bringing the country into the situation where it has now become the second largest economy in the world and one of the most important engines of the world economy, bringing millions of its own people out of poverty in the process. The collapse of the international export market has, however, placed China in a new situation, in which it must adopt new attitudes and new policies to confront the "new normal" of the world economy.

In this "new normal," Xi explained, many of the industries that have been the motor of the Chinese econ-

Purges during the cultural revolution.

Institute of Plasma Physics CAS

President Xi Jinping inspected the Institute of Plasma Physics Chinese Academy of Sciences

Institute of Plasma Physics CAS

omy will disappear or shift to a higher level of technology and productivity. Other industries will have to be developed that correspond with the growing needs of the country and the world. But the underlying dynamic force of the economy, President Xi argues, must now be situated in a process of making significant breakthroughs in science and technological innovation.

President Xi on Creativity

In one key section of his speech, President Xi expands on this notion. "Since the Sixteenth Century, mankind entered into an unprecedented period of scientific creativity," Xi writes. "In the course of a few hundred years, mankind achieved creative results which went far beyond anything that had been achieved in the previous thousands of years. Particularly since the Eighteenth Century, the world has experienced several scientific revolutions, more recently with developments in physics, the development of the steam engine and mechanical devices, electric power, the development of mass transport, the theory of relativity and quantum theory, an understanding of the electron, and the development of information technology. With these developments the world has experienced several scientific revolutions, such as mechanization, electrification, automation and informationization. And each of these profoundly changed the face and the pattern of human development."

"Some countries," he noted, "grasped the opportunity of the scientific revolution to put their economies into the 'fast lane,' with England becoming the chief beneficiary of the first industrial revolution, placing it in the role of a world leader. The second industrial revolution was grabbed by the United States, which soon replaced Great Britain's role in the world economy."

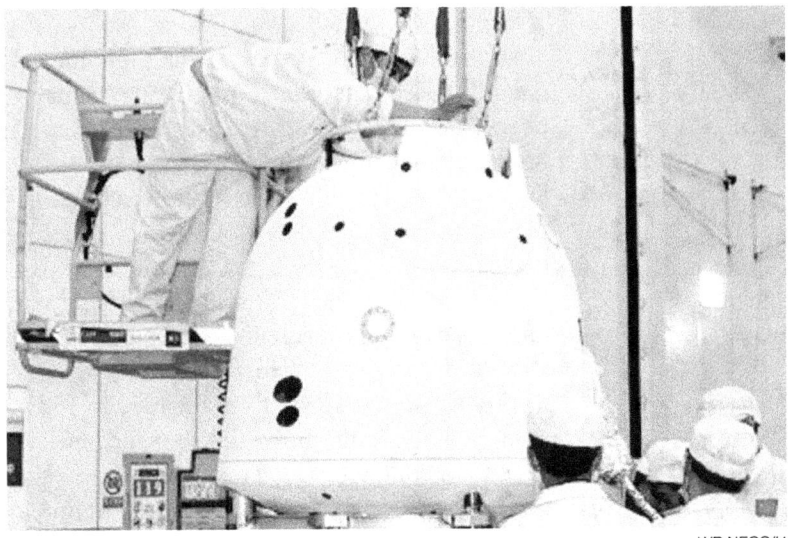

Chang'e 5-T1's re-entry module after vacuum thermal tests.

WP:NFCC#4

The Chinese people, Xi noted, are also a creative people and once played the foremost role in science and technology, particularly in the areas of astronomy, mathematics, agronomy, geography, and medicine, and gave the world those three great inventions: gunpowder, the art of printing, and the compass. "Some data show," Xi said, "that prior to the Sixteenth Century, among the 300 most important items of invention and discovery, 173 came from China, far exceeding those of Europe."

"For a long time our country played a leading role. Our thought, our social system, our economy, and our scientific achievements radiated strongly in our periphery and played a leading role there. And then in more recent years our country gradually lost its lead and plunged into backwardness. A major reason for this is that we lost the initiative several times in the scientific and industrial revolutions around us."

What this means for the present, Xi said, is that China must grasp the opportunity to move forward and moving forward means keeping on the cusp of creative innovation. "Only those who move ahead in innovating can maintain the ability to determine their own development," Xi said. He noted that we are facing another revolution in scientific and industrial development. While China has emerged as the number two economic power, that power is still quite fragile and facing major hurdles. For this reason, he urged a heightened awareness of the pitfalls ahead, noting that there is no clear roadmap, but that only a spirit of creativity and innovation on the part of the scientific elites and of the party

cadre will allow China to move ahead in these uncertain circumstances.

"Bringing forth new ideas is a complex process of social engineering," he said, "involving every section of the economy. To strengthen the development of creativity and innovation, you must insist on a holistic point of view, and seek to grasp the crucial elements, using the most important areas and key segments in order to create a breakthrough in the overall situation."

The emphasis on creativity and innovation has become a clarion call for China's economy. It indicates that only through breakthroughs in science and technology can China overcome its present bottlenecks and begin to raise the rest of its population to the standard of living now achieved by most of those concentrated in the urban core of the country.

With that in mind Xi urged the party cadre to increase their vigilance and commitment to the well-being of the people. Here also he called for creative solutions on the part of the party cadre to overcome the obstacles they find along the way. He underlined the need for a more intensive study of philosophy and the social sciences. While he underlined the role of Marxism and dialectical thought to these party members, he also referenced the importance of the Confucian values in formulating policy. He again noted that his anti-corruption campaign was initiated precisely in order to enhance the moral and social commitment of the party cadre, who are to serve as models for the type of social consciousness that he hopes to achieve in society as a whole, and he said the program was not some sort of American-style "House of Cards" manipulation, as it has been generally described by the Western media.

Lyndon LaRouche Responds

Lyndon LaRouche, while noting the importance of the orientation raised by the Chinese President, insisted that what was said was not sufficient. "Where does reality lie?" LaRouche asked. "Where does the reality of the human being, the human population, where does the destiny of mankind lie?"

The essence of the thing, and everybody who has made this particular mistake, has always paid a big price for it, if they were even able to survive.

Albert Einstein

CC/Informiguel Carreño

Because the question of what human values are, lies not in popular ideas. Not at all! It lies in something which is the *un*-popular idea.

You know, when you say the parents are proud of their children, or things like that, this sort of thing, this may have an inkling of some useful function; but the *idea* of it as a policy for people is wrong. It does not work. And we have not really grappled with this thing, we didn't want to grapple with it. Most people did *not* want to grapple with it! The point is, the secret of the future generation lies in a layer of society which did not play a role in what we call education today, and behavior today. Because it is the mind of the individual human, not as an educated individual as such, but it has to be the education within the person which enables that person to see beyond popular opinion. What does that mean? You say, well, look at the Twentieth Century, and most people don't realize how they were taken in, by the Twentieth Century: Why? Because the great geniuses were never heard, or almost never heard. Because the genius is one who is not developed to follow a certain pattern; the genius is someone who stands outside all notions of popular opinion, like Einstein.

Einstein is a prototype of what the future mankind, as an individual, represents. Other people don't. The objective is not to try to produce new children, made in the image of their parents. That is not the image, that is not the truth! That's the ugly truth, which is not the truth.

The point is, that Einstein one century after his death, has been noted for creativity. How did this work? How could Einstein, having no period of life from the time of his own actual death, how did he suddenly become a source of true creativity of a new generation? How! By being like Einstein; they do not base themselves on practicality. They base themselves on being *free* of the achievements of their families. If you want to succeed, *don't adopt your parents' habits.* And the future of mankind lies precisely in that policy. Because people collect ideas, trades, impulses, habits, all these kinds of things. And they all say "Ahh! I want to imitate this guy. I want to imitate this guy! I want to imitate this guy. I don't want to imitate this guy, I want to imitate somebody else." And that is how mankind degenerates, by trying to find a practical model, to recommend to all people in the organization, whatever the organization is, and that is how the 20th century was created, by the evil Bertrand Russell.

Later in the discussion, LaRouche elaborated on this point with regard to the space program:

What I'm talking about is the fact that mankind is not limited to mankind. That when people are landing on the Moon, such as is going to be done, what are you going to do? You're going to develop a Moon, but you don't know where the center lies, you don't know where the center is located. So therefore, you're going to rely upon something which has nothing in direct representation to what you're going to do on that Moon.

Now, the same thing came up earlier in the development of the whole system, and therefore you don't do it, you don't do it because you have to look for *something which is something that you have never defined.* And you're going to find a solution, experimentally you're going to find a solution, for something which has never been defined. And that's what the whole Moon program is, for the space program. It's a copy in effect, of exactly what the original space program was, as an experimental program.

In other words what you're getting, coming up from the Moon program, implicitly, will be something which has never happened, to any body known to mankind. It will be a different kind of body. And its implicit, because when you get this idea of how you're going to define the pattern of functioning, you don't know! Right, as of now, you don't know what will work. And what they will do—like the earlier founders of the program did, the same thing—they're going to have to find out something that they didn't know, and bring something that they had not known into play, and to verify that that thing *does* play.

The future of mankind lies with the person, whom the popular opinion *rejects*. And the reason for his success is he's right. And that's the model of man that we have to develop. This is the new model of man, who has, with some copies from the past as models, the ability to reject popular opinion. And reject it by throwing it in the garbage pail. And then throwing the garbage pail away, itself.

The future of mankind lies with a human being who is not so stupid as to copy what is already being done. And that is my slogan, and it has been my slogan for most of my life. Practically all of my life.

No, that's where the big problem is in society today, the culture of society. *The idea of trying to take a standard model of progress is absolutely*

V.I. Vernadsky

nonsense. It's absolutely dangerous. And that's where this organization often makes its most prominent mistakes, by trying to develop and produce a standard model.

We have to think more clearly than we have been thinking in some recent times. We have to realize that we are going into what seems to be the unknown, and you have to *accept the unknown*, accept it on a basis of its justice. But don't try to do something which you can copy from something else. You've got to find something that other people haven't discovered yet....

And the key thing I would re-emphasize is, *always make sure that you rely on something that you didn't believe before.* That's what makes it work. Our best generals always did that. They never did what popular opinion demanded. If you're practical, you're stupid, that's the general conclusion that comes out of that.

LaRouche's urgent intervention on the matter of creativity is particularly relevant for China at its present stage of development. As President Xi Jinping is clearly aware, the way forward for China is totally dependent on how quickly it can master the scientific problems facing it today. The future of energy, for instance, is in the long term, totally dependent on how quickly mankind can master the use of thermonuclear fusion power. And the source of that mastery is ultimately dependent on how quickly it can develop and nurture those individuals who will become tomorrow's Einsteins or Vernadskys. In that respect, the charge by Lyndon LaRouche, the world's premier economist, to *always make sure that you rely on something that you didn't believe before,* can only serve as crucial food for thought for Chinese thinkers who are today grappling with that problem.

Breakthrough on the Gulf of Oman: Big Step To Link Asia and Europe

by Ramtanu Maitra

May 28—On May 23, the Prime Minister of India and the Presidents of Afghanistan and Iran signed a trilateral agreement in Tehran, to develop Chabahar Port on the Gulf of Oman, in the southeastern Iranian province of Sistan-Balochistan. The agreement has been labeled "historic" and a "milestone." Subsequently, Iranian President Dr. Hassan Rouhani welcomed the agreement, saying,

> [T]his is a very important day for Iranians, and from now on it is going to be even more important, because today is going to mark the day of cooperation between three of us, Iran, India, and Afghanistan, and from now on this day can be called the day of Chabahar Of course the symbol of such cooperation *is* Chabahar, and 'Bahar' means spring, and it is a spring for the three of us.

But it is not only a "spring" for the three countries that signed the agreement. The project opens up a vast potential to make Central Asia a hub of development.

There is also no doubt that what Dr. Rouhani said on that occasion is at the heart of this agreement. The development of Chabahar Port and its free-trade zone, along with a 500 kilometer rail link between Chabahar and Zahedan, an Iranian city close to its borders with Pakistan and Afghanistan, has the potential to benefit all three countries immensely. A highway linking Zahedan and Zaranj, a town in Afghanistan's Nimruz province, already exists.

These projects, when completed, will provide Iran an opportunity to develop its sparsely populated and underdeveloped Sistan-Baluchistan province to grow and prosper, enable industrial development in the free-trade zone, and ease pressures on Iran's already crowded Bandar Abbas (Port Abbas) on the Strait of Hormuz, about 700 kilometers west of Chabahar. They will also strengthen Iran's trade and economic cooperation with India and Afghanistan in the coming years. In essence, Iran's long-term plans ensure that Chabahar Port will become a transit hub for immediate access to markets in the northern region of the Indian Ocean and in Central Asia.

From India's point of view also, the agreement is "historic." India has never before agreed to invest in such large-scale infrastructure development beyond its own borders. Chabahar Port will help India bypass Pakistan and open up a route to landlocked Afghanistan with which New Delhi has close security ties and shared economic interests. Moreover, it will allow India to trade effectively with all of Central Asia by sea and

land. Pakistan has not allowed India access to Afghanistan or Central Asia through its territory.

The development of Chabahar Port will also cut transportation time and costs between Iran and India's western ports by almost a third. Moreover, the access to Chabahar Port, and Zahedan and Zaranj further north, will allow India to reach four major Afghan cities—Kabul, Kandahar, Herat, and Mazar-e-Sharif—that are linked by Afghanistan's Garland Highway. India had already built the 220 kilometer Zaranj-Delaram highway within Afghanistan, known as Route 606, in 2009, which connects with the Garland Highway at Delaram.

For Afghanistan, this development could be a life saver. Over the last four decades, Afghanistan has been battered by foreign invasions that created armed insurgents—now organized as the Taliban—and made Afghanistan the prime center of world opium and heroin production. This process not only made the country highly insecure, but allowed a pall of hopelessness to set in. Recent reports indicate that thousands of Afghan youths are leaving the country, at a time when the presence of foreign armies in the country is bringing in more terrorists and jihadis from abroad, threatening a state of perpetual instability.

The Chabahar Port development will provide Kabul the opportunity to interact with the growth centers of Asia, and will also enable Indian Ocean countries, and even East Asian countries, to invest in Afghanistan and start the process of its stabilization. Iran's and India's hands-on involvement, via the transport corridor facilitated by the port development, could usher in the hope of Afghanistan becoming a mining and industrial nation in the decades ahead, instead of remaining the victim of London's geopolitical intrigues.

Putting Iran's Natural Gas to Work

The May 23 agreement—signed by Iran's President Dr. Hassan Rouhani, Indian Prime Minister Narendra Modi, and Afghanistan's President Ashraf Ghani—is extensive. But at the center is the development of Chabahar Port, the starting point. "The bilateral agreement to develop the Chabahar Port and related infrastructure, and the availability of about $500 million from India for this purpose, is an important milestone," Modi said in addressing the media jointly with Rouhani on May 23, India's PTI reported.

Beyond the port itself, India's Road Transport, Highways and Shipping Minister Nitin Gadkari, who accompanied Modi on this occasion, told PTI that "over Rs 1 trillion [about $16 billion] investment can happen in the Chabahar free trade zone." Iran, Gadkari said, has cheap natural gas and power, which Indian firms are keen to tap to build a half-million ton aluminum smelter and urea manufacturing units for nitrogen fertilizer. "We spend Rs 450 billion [about $7 billion] annually on a urea subsidy, and if we can manufacture it in the Chabahar free trade zone and move it through the port to Kandla [on the Indian coastal state of Gujarat] and onward to the hinterland, we can save that amount," he said. The Indian minister added that Indian aluminum manufacturer Nalco will set up the smelter, while private and cooperative fertilizer firms are keen to build urea plants. The railway public sector unit IRCON will build a rail line from Chabahar to move goods up to Afghanistan, Gadkari said. He said that India Ports Global Pvt, a joint venture of the Jawaharlal Nehru Port Trust and the Kandla Port Trust, will invest $85 million to develop two 640 meter container berths and three multi-cargo berths.

More than Commerce

While these major projects—to which Prime Minister Modi has committed for early implementation—will boost economic growth in the region, the closer cooperation among Iran, India, and Afghanistan will also link major countries across the Eurasian landmass. Re-establishing the direct links that were disrupted by the colonial British Raj and further weakened later by the Cold War geopolitics of the West, will allow the dormant cultural interactions between eastern parts of Asia and Central Asia to flourish once again. Referring to historical ties between India and Iran at a conference titled, "India and Iran, Two Great Civilizations: Retrospect and Prospects," on May 23 in Tehran, Modi said, "in the world of today, political pundits talk of strategic convergence. But India and Iran are two civilizations that celebrate the meeting of our great cultures. India and Iran have always been partners and friends. Our historical ties may have seen their share of ups and downs. But throughout, our partnership has remained a source of boundless strength for both of us," PTI reported from Tehran.

Prior to the conference, Prime Minister Modi released a facsimile edition of a rare Persian manuscript of the *Kalileh-wa-Dimneh*, a translation of the *Panchatantra* and the *Jataka* tales, to highlight the centuries-old close cultural ties between India and Iran. He said,

narendramodi.in

Indian Prime Minister Narendra Modi presents the facsimile edition of the Kalileh-wa-Dimneh *at the conference on "India and Iran, Two Great Civilizations," May 23 in Tehran.*

It is remarkable how the simple stories of the Indian classics of *Jataka* and *Panchatantra* became the Persian *Kalileh-wa-Dimneh*. It is a classic example of exchange and travel of cultural ideas between two societies—a beautiful demonstration of how our two cultures and countries think alike.

He called it "a true depiction of the wisdom of our ancient civilizations."

The *Jataka* tales, dated between 300 BC and 400 AD, form a part of the canon of sacred Buddhist literature. This collection of some 550 anecdotes and fables depicts earlier incarnations of the future Buddha, Siddhartha Gautama. Buddha is considered by the Hindus—and was acknowledged by Siddhartha himself—to be an incarnation of the Indian God Vishnu. Many of the Jataka tales are set in or near Varanasi, a sacred city of the Hindus located in north central India on the Ganges, in the political constituency of Prime Minister Modi.

Kalileh-wa-Dimneh was first written in Pahlavi, the Persian language of the Sassanid era (224-651 AD). The first five chapters are from the Sanskrit book, *Panchatantra*, which provides *hitopadesh* (Sanskrit for "good advice") to a king, through the mouths of animals. Scholars point out that when, in the Sixth Century, the Sassanid King Khosru Nushrivan learned that there was a Sanskrit book that advises kings, he sent a Sanskrit-Persian scholar to India to obtain a copy and

translate it. Later, in the Eighth Century, Ibn al-Mokaffa translated it into Arabic, and it is considered a classic of Arabic literature. In many Arab countries, textbooks carry these tales.

Responding to Modi's highlighting of the India-Iran traditional and cultural relationship in the past, President Rouhani said India's relationship with Iran today starts with Chabahar, "but its end will be an all-out comprehensive development, and economic and cultural cooperation."

The Wider Regional Connectivity

The development of Chabahar Port and the linking of Chabahar to Zahedan will put in place an eastern leg of the International North South Transport Corridor (INSTC). This eastern leg will link Iran and Afghanistan to South Asia, Southeast Asia, East Asia, and China by land and sea. The western or main leg of the INSTC—a multi-modal transportation route officially agreed upon in the year 2000 by Iran, Russia, and India at a meeting in St. Petersburg—is designed to link South Asia and some ports of Southeast Asian nations, to Europe and Central Asia via the Indian Ocean, the Persian Gulf, and the Caspian region. It runs through Iran and Azerbaijan, and then through the Russian Federation to northern Europe.

Connecting this eastern leg with the main INSTC, however, will require an adequate link from Zahedan to Tehran. Iran's work on this route is still in its early stages.

The main INSTC route itself is not quite complete, because one section of railroad is still being built. However, a dry run of this route was successfully conducted by the Federation of Freight Forwarders of India in 2014. One benefit of this trial run was that it established the extent of the large savings of this route when compared to the Suez Canal-Mediterranean route to Europe (see map, next page).

As of now, the Asian trade travelling via the main INSTC unloads at Bandar Abbas and then goes by rail to Tehran and Qazvin, thence by road to Bandar Anzali (Port Anzali) to be loaded onto a ship crossing the Caspian Sea from south to north. It arrives at Astrakhan in the Russian Federation, where it is unloaded and re-

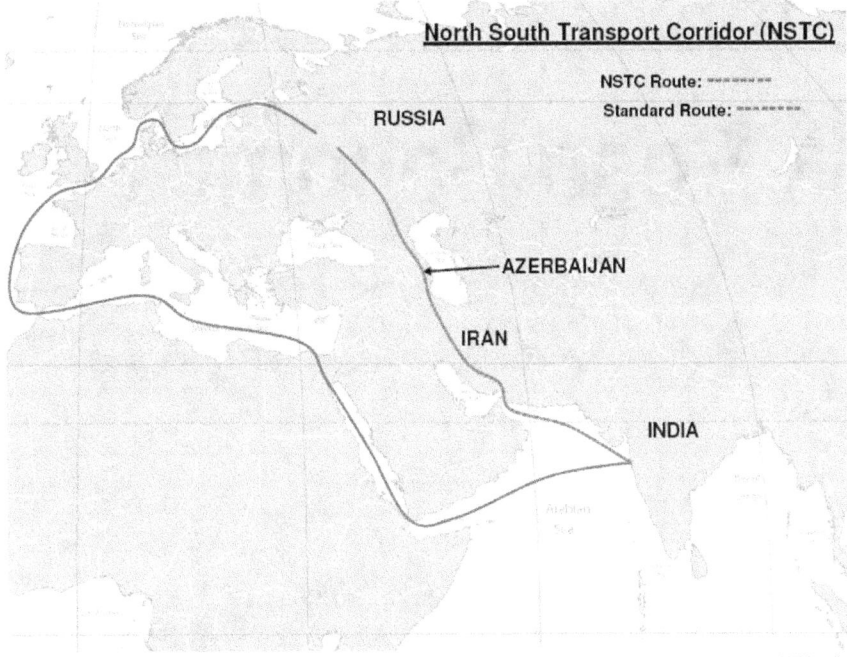

North South Transport Corridor (NSTC)

NSTC Route: ------
Standard Route: --------

RUSSIA

AZERBAIJAN

IRAN

INDIA

From South Asia to Europe: the International North-South Transport Corridor (red) and the old route (blue).

nation Committee has pushed all parties to provide a competitive route from Asia to Europe through an efficient cooperation. ...

The train departed from the northwest of China, from Shihezi city in the Xinjiang Uyghur Autonomous Region, on July 28, and arrived at Alat Port (Baku) in six days. The train, which consists of 82 containers and 41 platforms, traveled 4000 km and stopped in Aktau Port in Kazakhstan. Multimodal transport is the key point here, which links Aktau with the Port of Baku through rail ferries. Although it requires time to transport trains via rail ferries, the Trans Caspian route shortens the time and distance between China and Europe.

The Institute, based in Istanbul, is devoted to the Caspian region.

loaded to travel by rail to northern Europe. That is how the route operates now.

But within three years, there will be a major improvement in efficiency. Iran is building a railroad from Qazvin to Rasht through a mountain pass, to bring the route to the southwestern corner of the Caspian Sea, and will then extend it along the western shore of the Caspian to Astara, bordering Azerbaijan. From Astara, cargo will travel on the existing Azerbaijan-Russian Federation railroad through Baku (Azerbaijan).

The INSTC enables a south-north transport corridor through which countries on the Indian Ocean littoral can trade through Iran into Europe, and also into Central Asia via Afghanistan. At the same time, another connection is developing that will link China to Central Asia and beyond toward Europe, through the Caspian Sea. One could call this an east-west transport corridor. Seray Özkan of the Hazar Strategic Institute reported, Aug. 27, 2015:

On August 3, 2015, the first cargo [test] train from China arrived at Baku International Sea Trade Port (Port of Baku) in Azerbaijan. It was the first successful attempt to launch a cargo train from China to the Caspian Region through the Caspian Sea. There have been efforts to utilize this route; especially the Trans-Caspian Coordi-

III. Alexander Hamilton and Manhattan

Alexander Hamilton's Challenge To Us Today

"Alexander Hamilton created the schedule of the World"
—Lyndon LaRouche, May 14, 2016

by Robert Ingraham

Preface: Why Do We Study History?

Why publish an article of this type, at this moment, on the subject of Alexander Hamilton? Certainly not because he is the subject of a hit Broadway musical. Nor simply because we are desperately in need of a revival of Hamilton's economic policies. It is the world crisis today, the life or death reality of the current threat of world war and and the destruction of humanity, that impels this effort.

We must act to overcome the threats we are facing. We must have solutions. But not just any action, not just any solution. In reality, no "set solution" of any type will work under the current circumstances. No "program" will work. Fighting simply "to win" also will not work. Seemingly insurmountable crises, seemingly immovable obstacles, can only be defeated by bringing into existence something new, something revolutionary, something unexpected.

In 1789 Friedrich Schiller—in a piece titled, "What Is, and to What End, Do We Study Universal History?"—wrote:

> Only from history will you learn to set a value on the goods from which habit and unchallenged possession so easily deprive us of our gratitude; priceless, precious goods, to which the blood of the best and the most noble clings, goods which had to be won by the hard work of so many generations! And who among you, in whom a bright spirit is conjugated with a

Friedrich Schiller, shown in conversation, dealt with the questions: What is History? And why should it be studied?

feeling heart, could bear this high obligation in mind, without a silent wish being aroused in him to pay that debt to coming generations which he can no longer discharge to those past? A noble desire must glow in us to also make a contribution out of our means to this rich bequest of truth, morality, and freedom which we received from the world past, and which we must surrender once more, richly enlarged, to the world to come, and, in this eternal chain which winds itself through all human generations, to make firm our ephemeral existence. However different the destinies may be which await you in society, all of you can contribute something to this! A path toward immortality has been opened up to every achievement, to the true immortality, I mean, where the deed lives and rushes onward, even if the name of the author should remain behind.

But where is to be found that "noble desire" of which Schiller speaks? How might we make those vital "contributions" that he proposes? By what means, and through the mobilization of what innate powers, shall we secure a better future for humanity? It is only in attempting to answer those questions that one can legitimately approach the life of Alexander Hamilton, and in so doing, discover clues—a beacon—which might guide us through the battle in which we are today engaged.

oil portrait by Daniel Huntington.

Alexander Hamilton, shown here, created the American Republic.

the willingness to challenge and fight against great odds for the truthfulness of a creative insight, and for the implications of what that insight portends for future generations, for yet unborn human beings. Real creativity always derives from a vision of future potential motivating one's actions in the present.

History is not the study of past events. It is an investigation into those singular creative discoveries which have advanced the potential for the continuation and accelerated development of the human species; discoveries which provide a glimpse into the unlocking of pre-existing but as yet unknown truths, into the meaning of the birth of human beings; discoveries which create new universes for human habitation.

Such discoveries are rare, and they always go against majority opinion, against the prevailing culture and beliefs of society. They are always a minority view. And they must be vigorously defended.

It is only through reflection, through a somber appreciation of this question—of the role of the individual creative human personality, of the creation of the seemingly impossible—that one is able to begin an inquiry into the life of Alexander Hamilton. Hamilton *created* the American Republic—an entirely new potential for the human species—and it is in contemplating the quality of the mind that brought that creation into existence, that insights may be gained as to what is required of us if we are to win the battle in which we are today engaged.

On May 10, 2016, Lyndon LaRouche delivered an historic presentation to a group of associates at his home in Virginia. We will return to its profound implications throughout this present article. For now, a few short excerpts from that talk will suffice to situate the necessary approach:

It comes in the ability of mankind, to develop within the human individual the characteristics to

Introduction: On Creativity

It would be wrong to describe Alexander Hamilton, or any other truthfully creative individual, as embodying a "combination" of creativity and courage. For real creativity—not the existential nonsense that passes for creativity today—is, in and of itself, a courageous act, give a higher degree of power to mankind as a whole, through self-development of the human species. That's the *only* thing that is important …

The issue is, can the human species produce from within its own ranks a body of people who will meet the challenge of defeating the kind of evil we have to face now …

Creativity is the battlefield—precisely because creativity, properly understood, is the fight for the future. It is a fight to unlock secrets that will give new meaning to man's role in the universe. Real creativity is a war, stemming from a desire to challenge backward, defective axioms that have been imposed on society, whether that imposition originates with the forces of empire and oligarchy, or the depravity of the existing culture. Real creativity involves the willingness to fight, against great odds, to achieve a breakthrough for the benefit of future humanity. Such was Wilhelm Furtwángler's confrontation with Adolph Hitler. Such was Douglas MacArthur's de-

EIRNS/Stuart Lewis

Lyndon H. LaRouche, Jr.

cision at Inchon. That is how history is made. All great creative personalities operate within the realm of *great strategic flanks.*

I. The Creation

In that same May 10 address, LaRouche stated, "The desire is not to win, the desire is to create. And to do nothing that does not allow you to create."

Thus do we begin our examination into the life of Alexander Hamilton.

Why one child develops into a creative personality, a world-historical figure, and another does not, is a question that, as yet, is still beyond our full comprehension. In Alexander Hamilton's case, some things are known about his early life and upbringing, but the available scraps of information do not answer the question as to how and why he emerged as a force that changed the future of human society. To say that he received instructions from this or that teacher, or that he read certain books, is a paltry, reductionist approach that answers

painting by John Trumbull

General George Washington shown here at the time of his first farewell address, resigning his role as Commander in Chief of the Army, at Annapolis, Maryland in 1783.

White House Historical Association, by Rembrandt Peale   by Gilbert Stuart, at National Gallery of Art

Washington respected and trusted John Jay (center) and had a close relationship with Gouverneur Morris (right), but always looked to Hamilton for leadership, and never once sided with Jefferson (left) on any important issue.

nothing. Others had the same teachers; others read the same books, But they did not become a Hamilton.

What is known for certain is that from the moment he left adolescence, after his arrival in New York City in 1773, his very first public utterances, his very first writings, were devoted to the creation of something new, something never seen before in human society. He instantaneously became a passionate partisan for the American revolutionary cause, and the genius of the 18-year-old Hamilton was already displayed in his two writings of 1774, *A Full Vindication of the Measures of Congress* and *The Farmer Refuted*. Most telling is that, even in these youthful, inaugural works, the evidence of Hamilton's willingness to stand and fight for the truth against majority opinion is emphatically presented.

George Washington, in an act which speaks volumes about his own character, recognized the extraordinary nature of Hamilton's mind and personality from almost the moment he met him, and in 1777, the 19-year-old Hamilton became not simply Washington's *aide de camp*, but his most trusted and valued military adviser, a position which Hamilton would hold for four years.

Washington always supported Hamilton. He supported him at the Constitutional Convention of 1787. He supported his monumental economic revolution of 1790-1791. During the intense conflicts within his administration, Washington never once sided with Jefferson against Hamilton on any issue of importance. Washington trusted and respected John Jay, and his relationship with Gouverneur Morris was more familiar and personal, but *it was to the younger Hamilton that Washington always looked for leadership.*

Unlike the misguided populists and xenophobes of present day Europe and America, Alexander Hamilton was never tricked into merely fighting *against* someone or something; his was always an effort to give birth to great strategic flanks, always attacking, but doing so in a way that redefined the battle, under new rules of combat, and always developing new potentials for victory. Each breakthrough, each new flank, created new potencies within the population.

Birth of an Idea

The moment at which Hamilton perceived the *historic potential* of the American Revolution can not be known, but it is certain that from a very early date, Hamilton had a singular conception of what needed to be brought into existence, what could and must be created. Many people took part in the American Revolution, and of those, many things could be said, both noble and profane. What is clear, is that no one—as is shown conclusively in the proceedings of the 1787 Constitutional Convention—grasped the implications of the momentous "historic opportunity," except for Hamilton.

Earlier, in 1781, Hamilton had taken two actions, and everything that was to develop later, emerged from these two initiatives. On April 30, he authored a lengthy essay, which he sent as a letter to the financier Robert Morris, in which he put forward a proposal for the establishment of a National Bank and a National Credit System. Several months later, he delivered a proposal to the New York State legislature calling for the convening of a national convention for the purpose of rectifying the miserable failings and shortcomings of the Articles of Confederation. This began the process that would lead to the convening of the Constitutional Convention in the summer of 1787.

These were not two separate initiatives, but two derived products of one idea, one creative thrust, intended to bring into being a sovereign constitutional republic, a republic with the power to defend itself against the rapacious and oligarchical governments of Europe; a republic intended to exhibit in its very nature a dedication to developing in each individual citizen a republican culture; a republic charged to act and to foster the *potential* for the further advance of the condition of the human species.

These were not simply economic and constitutional proposals for the creation of certain types of institutions; rather, the intent was to define a new dynamic within human society that would to advance the human identity. This was to be a republic based on the principle of human potential and human progress. Most emphatically, Hamilton's dedication to using the power of the republic to engender rapid advances in scientific and technological discoveries, and to establish both a constitution and a credit system to advance that progress, defined a very specific insight into the paramount importance of the issue of human culture.

Historians and biographers usually treat personages such as Hamilton by trying to prove that all of their ideas derived from something in the past. They will say, "Hamilton's ideas on constitutional law came from his study of British legal theory," or "Hamilton's theories on trade derived from his study of Grotius." Such "historians" are incapable of grasping the creation of something that is *new*, something that overturns all previously accepted axioms.

The adoption of the Constitution in 1787, followed by Hamilton's 1790-1791 economic initiatives, were all part of one revolution: the creation and future development of the new republic. The adoption of the Constitution made possible the history-changing economic revolution which followed. It was one revolution, one creation, one intention, a singular but multiply-connected idea, as it flowed from Hamilton's mind.

I ask the reader to consider all of this as we proceed. What follows must necessarily include much historical detail, and it is easy to get lost in the details. Bear in mind that everything discussed below must be situated in what has just been presented.

The Constitution

The American Constitution was entirely the creation of Alexander Hamilton. There would not even

have been a Convention but for Hamilton. Following his 1781 proposal to the New York legislature, Hamilton authored his six *Continentalist* essays arguing for the power of the national government to develop the future economic potential of the nation. In July 1782, at his urging, the New York legislature adopted a resolution, calling for the convening of a national convention to overhaul the Articles of Confederation. In November 1792, Hamilton was elected to the national Congress in Philadelphia. There he wrote papers, delivered speeches, and introduced resolutions calling for a convention. In 1783 he authored yet another resolution, this one including an outline for an entirely new National Constitution, *an outline very similar to the proposal that he later put forth at the Philadelphia Convention in 1787.* This was the idea, the germ, from which everything later flowed.

Then, two crucial meetings followed in 1785 and 1786. In March 1785 the Mount Vernon Conference was held at the Virginia home of George Washington. In September 1786, the Annapolis Convention was held in Annapolis, Maryland. Both meetings were convened to deal with shortcomings in the Articles of Confederation, particularly in regard to interstate trade and other economic matters. The scope of the agenda for the two meetings was very limited, and the thinking of most of the delegates even more limited. But for Hamilton, who was a delegate to the Annapolis Convention, this meeting became a moment of historically specific opportunity. It was a moment in which, in the words of LaRouche, "an individual of principle outmaneuvered the practicality of everyone else."

Hamilton convinced the assembled delegates that something greater than a few patchwork reforms was needed, and at the conclusion of the discussions, the convention unanimously adopted what became known as the *Annapolis Resolution*, a declaration—authored by Hamilton and sent to the national Congress in Philadelphia as well as to all of the thirteen state governments—calling for the convening of a national constitutional convention. That convention met in June.

On June 18, 1787, Alexander Hamilton delivered a six-hour speech to the assembled delegates at the Convention in Philadelphia. That speech, more than any other specific initiative that one could name, gave birth to the United States. Historians like to point to the Virginia Plan of James Madison as the basis for what became the final form of the Constitution. That is absurd! For Madison and the Virginia slaveholders, the Constitution was never more than a social contract, with no moral imperative. The Virginia Plan was not a constitution; by maintaining "states' rights," it perpetuated an agrarian, slavery-dominated, purposeless society. Without a national mission, heteronomy and greed would have been the primary social dynamic in such a future society. Any contrary analysis of what transpired at the Philadelphia Convention comes from the damaged imaginations of individuals who fail miserably to comprehend the nature of the *mind* of Hamilton and what it was that *he* was determined to create.

Jefferson's cousin, Edmund Randolph, shown here, was Attorney General of the United States.

Earlier articles in *EIR* have made the case that the American Revolution was not a mere "tax revolt," that it was not simply a rebellion against "big government" oppression. But for Thomas Jefferson, the southern slave-mongers, and many others, that is exactly what it was! "Get the government off our backs! Let us whip our slaves and distill our whiskey in peace"—the later secessionist Confederacy's notion of Freedom. It was Hamilton, at Philadelphia, who determined that we would not go down that road.

The details of the fight at the Constitutional Convention have been reported elsewhere,[1] and they need not be repeated here, but it is necessary to be clear that it was Hamilton, together with Gouverneur Morris and very few others, who established both the Office of the Presidency, with broad implied powers, and a powerful national judiciary. It was Hamilton who embedded the concept of the *General Welfare* in the Constitution and who gave the Constitution its intent—of developing the nation for *posterity*—thus imbuing the entire document and the future republic

itself with a purpose, a truly revolutionary mission.

The Revolution

The successful ratification of the Constitution in 1788 was the indispensable victory which then made possible entirely new flanks for the unfolding of the full revolution. In the 24-month period of 1790 and 1791, Treasury Secretary Hamilton authored four reports for the new administration of George Washington. These were the *First Report on the Public Credit* (January 14, 1790), the *Report on a National Bank* (December 14, 1790), the *Report on the Establishment of a Mint* (January 28, 1791), and the *Report on Manufactures* (December 5, 1791). All four of these, taken together, created a whole—a unified principle and policy for the development of the nation, and the transformation of the opportunities and skills, and the cognitive development, of the population. Nothing like this had ever been witnessed before in human history.

This was not a linear extension of any past economic or governmental system. It was not a "republic" of the Venetian or Dutch variety. It was a revolutionary change in the underlying dynamic of society, all flowing from a precise intention to create a *possibility* for the uplifting and improvement of the human species.

Thomas Jefferson and James Madison went wild. In 1789, they had believed, or at least hoped, that their faction might come to dominate the Washington Administration. Jefferson was Secretary of State. His cousin, the Virginian Edmund Randolph, was Attorney General. The slave states held a majority in the House of Representatives, with Madison as their spokesman. Jefferson did not know Hamilton at all, and as for Madison and the rest of the slave-owners' faction, they vastly underestimated the personality they were up against. Hamilton

James Madison was spokesman for the slavocracy. He and Jefferson fought Hamilton's National Bank proposal.

1. See Robert Ingraham, "Manhattan's Struggle for Human Freedom Against the Slave Power of Virginia," *EIR*, May 8, 2015.

turned the tables on all of them. In military terms, his Four Reports and what they implied, routed the fixed positions of his enemies and created an open field for the intended transformation to proceed.

Jefferson and Madison struck back. They charged that Hamilton, in his proposal for a National Bank, was attempting to overthrow the Constitution, and that the National Government had no power to intervene in the freedom of the marketplace. Jefferson lobbied Washington intensely against the proposal. On February 23, 1791, Hamilton responded with his *Opinion on the Constitutionality of a National Bank*, and two days later George Washington signed the law to establish the Bank of the United States.

In December 1791, Hamilton broke through on another flank with the publication of his *Report on Manufactures*. That report took what was implied and made possible by the first two reports, to its necessary conclusion—that is, the utilization of a national Credit System to unleash the creative and inventive potentials of the American people, and to affirm the power and responsibility of the sovereign government to direct such a revolution in industry and science.

These were not "economic policies"! An entirely new culture was to be nurtured, a new sense of identity, a new, higher morality, wherein the productive powers and creative potential of each citizen would become the standard for true value—this would become the *very nature* of the nation itself.

In his address on May 10, Lyndon LaRouche said, "It's the development of the individual within the nation, that is the key to power. The ability to create something better than mankind has known and experienced beforehand." This is the precise—scientifically precise—intention and dynamic which Hamilton set into motion.

What Hamilton Wrought

Whither the United States? Whither the human species? Consider the history of the last 200 years—had Hamilton not lived. Look at what happened in India. Look at what happened in Africa. The deaths, the opium, the indescribable suffering. Lacking Hamilton's intervention, that would have been the future for all of us; humanity would have been crushed by the power of Empire. The British oligarchical system, and its depraved view of human nature, would have ruled unchal-

lenged for the entirety of the 19th Century.

That didn't happen. Such was Hamilton's victory. Such his strategic gift to humanity. Hamilton changed the future for the entire human species, and he did it by recognizing the potential for an entirely different future—and then risking everything to bring that better future into existence.

Most people view history as a series of battles between two opposing sides, a set piece battle, like a chessboard. Such adolescent notions are based on erroneous, simple-minded sense perception. As LaRouche has stressed, the issue is not one of winning, but of creating. A creative intervention destabilizes and disorients the enemy; it "sets them off their heels." And it creates the necessary space to bring in something *entirely new*, something which unlocks pre-existing but previously unrealized potentials for victory. After his death, Hamilton's Revolution was largely overthrown by the forces of Empire and the Slavocracy, but his victory *changed everything* in the world; it changed the world *forever*—and what he had unlocked, remained unlocked for all future generations.

II. Insurrection

In May 1791, Thomas Jefferson and James Madison traveled to New York City, and during the month of June they held several meetings with Robert Livingston and Aaron Burr. The subject of those discussions was a plot to bring about Hamilton's downfall, to reverse his policy initiatives, to drive him out of the Washington Administration, and to destroy him both politically and

Jefferson and Madison plotted unsuccessfully with Robert Livingston (left) and Aaron Burr (right) to bring about Hamilton's downfall.

personally. They adopted as their motto *"Delenda est Carthago"* (Carthage must be destroyed).

In the autumn of 1791 Jefferson began to establish a nationwide series of newspapers and journals with the intent of launching total war against Hamilton. One of the first of these, the *National Gazette*, was set up by Philip Freneau in Philadelphia, with direct financial support from Jefferson. Others, including the treasonous Philadelphia *Aurora*, soon followed.

The *raison d'être* behind the treason of the oligarchical Slavocracy was given away by Madison, in a January, 1792 letter to a colleague, wherein—in reaction to the just released *Report on Manufactures*—he wrote, "What do you think of the commentary on the terms *general welfare*? This broaches a new constitutional doctrine of vast consequence and demanding the serious attention of the public … If Congress can do whatever in their discretion can be done by money, and will promote the general welfare, the Government is no longer a limited one possessing enumerated powers, but an indefinite one …"

Thus the issue was made explicit: The General Welfare Principle as enunciated by Hamilton at the Philadelphia Convention—the principle which defined the *purpose* of the new nation—was named by Jefferson and Madison as the enemy. Hamilton's 1787-1791 creation of a Constitutional Republic and a National Credit System, and his intention to develop the power of the national culture was to be overthrown.

Throughout 1792 and 1793, efforts by the Slavocracy to drive Hamilton out of the government escalated. The details are extensive, but they culminated in Jefferson's deployment of Virginia Congressman William Branch Giles to introduce a resolution to remove Hamilton from office for "maladministration in the duties of his office," effectively an impeachment resolution. When this resolution was presented to the House on February 27, 1793, it received only five votes, including that of James Madison.

Unable to pry Washington loose from his alliance with Hamilton, Jefferson's next step was to launch a series of Jacobin organizations through which the Constitutional Republic might be overthrown. The method was to recruit individuals by appealing to their lowest,

Jefferson created Jacobin organizations to overthrow the Constitutional Republic. The first two were headed by John Peter Muhlenberg (left) and Alexander Dallas (right).

most base instincts of self-interest, avarice, rage, and fear. These organizations went under a variety of names, but the most common appellation was "Democratic Society." The first two originated in Philadelphia in the spring of 1793, headed by Peter Muhlenberg and Alexander Dallas. Within months, dozens more were set up throughout the nation. By 1794 these organizations were fully deployed in an onslaught to destroy Hamilton and overthrow Washington's government.

France and Its 'Revolution'

For Thomas Jefferson, the raper of slave women, his intention for the United States was always grounded in an abysmally depraved view of human nature. Freedom from the British was simply the freedom to unleash the inner beast, only constrained by the "rule of law" designed to keep the satiation of animal appetites within manageable boundaries.

After the storming of the Bastille in July 1789, revenge-mad mobs ran through the streets of Paris, their faces and clothes smeared with blood, carrying aloft pikes on which the heads of their victims were impaled. The horrified Gouverneur Morris, who witnessed these scenes, concluded at that very moment that—far from this being a replica of the American Revolution—a monumental evil had been unleashed. Thomas Jefferson, who was also in Paris at that time, shed crocodile tears over the "revolutionary excesses," but throughout the entirety of the 1790s, he repeatedly defended the continuing carnage as a necessary "bloodletting" of the revolution.

In 1798 Hamilton authored two articles, both under the title of *The Stand*. He wrote:

In reviewing the disgusting spectacle of the French Revolution, it is difficult to avert the eye entirely from those features of it which betray a plan to disorganize the human mind itself, as well as to undermine the venerable pillars that support the edifice of civilized society ...

It is not necessary to heighten the picture by sketching the horrid group of proscriptions and murders which have made France a den of pillage and slaughter; blackening with eternal opprobrium the very name of man ... The pious and moral weep over these scenes as a sepulcher destined to entomb all they revere and esteem. The politician who loves liberty, sees them with regret as a gulf that may swallow up the liberty to which he is devoted ...

For those who grew to maturity in the 1960s, the continuing heritage of what Hamilton describes should be all too familiar. The "revolutionary violence" of Frantz Fanon, the popularity of the film, *Battle of Algiers*, the prescription for human "happiness" defined by the Marquis de Sade—this is our inheritance from Thomas Jefferson and his allies among the *Montagnards*, the French faction that unleashed the Reign of Terror in 1794. This degradation of the human identity to the sensual abyss is still with us today. It is seen in the British- and Saudi-backed ISIS and Al-Nusra. It is also the beast which occupies the soul of Barack Obama, an individual whose identity as a youth was shaped by the participation of his father in the mass murder and torture of the Indonesian genocide of 1965-1966.

This heritage is also the pervasive reality of today's trans-Atlantic culture. It is not simply that Obama and other leaders murder people in cold blood; of far greater importance is a culture which tolerates this, a people who avert their eyes or protest ignorance. At the heart of this issue is a question: Is the nation, is our culture governed by a dynamic of destruction, or one of creation? "Revolutionary" France of the 1790s was rapidly devolving into what can only be described as a Nazi regime. It became explicit with the 1799 Coup of 18 *Brumaire*, which brought Napoleon Bonaparte to power. The true nature of this monstrosity—this unleashing of human depravity—is perhaps best understood by spending one or two hours studying what Francisco Goya presents in his *Los desastres de la Guerra*.

In the plethora of his writings during the 1790s, Hamilton returns again and again to the issue of the French Revolution. Central to everything he discusses is the human identity—and the extraordinary danger posed—by what was occurring in France—to the morality and self-conception of the American people. The perpetuation and further development of republican ideals is only possible through the development of the citizenry. That is the battleground.

During his May 10th address, Lyndon LaRouche discusses this question directly:

> Mankind is not a bunch of objects that you can manipulate and make the toys dance for you. That does not work. You have to actually create a power *in* mankind which is improved *over* previously existing expressions of mankind. That is the whole game. And you have to spread this kind of development, such that it sustains itself ...

During the 1790s, Jefferson and his coalition of plantation owners and financial speculators, imported the Satanic impulses of French Jacobinism into America to manipulate the passions, fears, and greed of Americans against Hamilton's revolution. Jefferson's method was to build a cadre of "enraged ones" (*Les Enragés*) who could be thrown against Hamilton and his allies. This southern culture of violence, racism, Jacobinism, and barbarity has always been the internal enemy of Hamilton's Republic. It was the well-spring of the Confederacy.[2] It was institutionalized with the creation of the FBI. And it is with us today.

Neutrality and the Jay Treaty

Jefferson's insurrection against Hamilton's leadership intensified, particularly after Washington's *Proclamation of Neutrality* in 1793 and the negotiation of the Jay Treaty with England in 1794, both of which were strongly urged on Washington by Hamilton and violently opposed by Jefferson and Madison.

The *Proclamation* was issued to forestall a nationwide mobilization by the Jefferson machine to drag the United States into a war with Britain as an ally of Maximilien Robespierre. Although the danger of war was real and urgent, there was also a more profound, *positive*, feature to the *Proclamation*; it defined an en-

_____

2. In 1861, prior to the later adoption of *Dixie*, the unofficial national anthem of the secessionists was *The Southern Marseillaise*, the French revolutionary song, set with new words. It was sung on the streets of Charleston, South Carolina, and New Orleans, Louisiana, by Confederate soldiers marching off to war.

tirely new approach to relations among nations. It introduced a new paradigm as to how human interaction on the planet would proceed. The *Proclamation* was unequivocal in stating that the United States would not be drawn into wars of rivalry between the European empires, that the killing and destruction on behalf of hereditary oligarchies which had dominated Europe for centuries would find no place in America. From the vantage-point of a republican culture, it avowed that it was the intention of the United States to maintain peace with all nations, a peace based on mutually beneficial trade and economic relations, and non-interference.

The Jay Treaty, negotiated one year later, was fully coherent in principle with the *Proclamation*. Its supreme accomplishment was in resolving all of the areas of conflict left over from the American Revolution, exactly those "danger points" which Jefferson and Madison were attempting to leverage to provoke a war with Britain.[3]

In reaction to these developments, frenzied violence—instigated by Jefferson's Democratic Societies—erupted all over the country. Philip Freneau, writing in the *Aurora*, charged that Washington wanted to enact the Jay Treaty to make himself a king: "His wishes will be gratified with a hereditary monarchy and a House of Lords." It was during this period that the Jeffersonians began publicly to attack Hamilton, Washington, Jay, and others as monarchists, and it must be understood that the label of *monarchist* in 1792 carried an even more sinister and deadly implication than being named a *communist* in 1952.

At this time Hamilton spoke openly to friends of the danger of civil war erupting. Oliver Wolcott, who had succeeded Hamilton as Treasury Secretary, agreed, writing to Hamilton, "I think we shall have no dangerous riots, but one month will determine the fate of our country."

In 1796, Washington released his (Hamilton-authored) *Farewell Address*, in which he reiterated the principle of Neutrality. The response to this speech by the minions of the Virginia slavocracy was venomous. One newspaper denounced Washington's words as "the loathings of a sick mind." In the *Aurora*, Benjamin Franklin Bache accused Washington of having conspired

---

3. In 1798, to forestall conflict with France, which would erupt into the Quasi-War, Hamilton urged President John Adams to negotiate a treaty with France, along the lines of the Jay Treaty, in order to preserve the peace.

with the British during the American Revolution. Thomas Paine penned an open letter to Washington, expressing the hope that Washington would die and telling him that "the world will be puzzled to decide whether you are an apostate or an impostor, whether you have abandoned good principles or whether you ever had any."

III. Counterattack

On January 26, 1795 Hamilton resigned his position as Treasury Secretary and left the Washington administration. His reasons for doing so were entirely financial and familial. By 1795, Hamilton and his wife had five children and were nearly impoverished after five years in government service. They owned little more than a few sticks of furniture, and he was deeply in debt. Jubilant over Hamilton's departure, Madison wrote, sneeringly, to Jefferson, "Hamilton will go to New York with the word *poverty* as his label."

But Madison would be forced to swallow his triumphant sneers, because it became very clear, very quickly, that Hamilton remained the leader of the Washington Administration. Washington wrote to him repeatedly for advice. Secretary of State Pickering, Secretary of War McHenry and, particularly, Secretary of Treasury Wolcott—with Washington's approval—all looked to Hamilton as the *de facto* leader of the Republic. Hamilton corresponded regularly with Washington, wrote speeches for him, and authored numerous articles and appeals that appeared in the press. As many of his contemporaries remarked at the time, the relationship between Washington and Hamilton actually deepened in its intimacy and mutual trust after Hamilton had left office.

After January 1795, Manhattan would serve as Hamilton's command center, the location from which he would defend his revolution and battle the growing political and cultural degeneration of the nation. By 1798 his ally John Jay was Governor of New York State; his collaborator Rufus King was there, his father-in-law Philip Schuyler was there, and in 1798 his friend Gouverneur Morris returned to New York from Europe. This was a New York-based effort to preserve Hamilton's Revolution for future generations.

Treason in High Places

By 1796, Washington was finished with Jefferson and his allies. The evidence of Jefferson's conspiracies was overwhelming, and Jefferson's agents, such as

New York Historical Society Museum and Library
Left: National Portrait Gallery, Washington D.C.

After he left the Washington Administration, Hamilton's close collaborators in New York, in addition to John Jay and Gouverneur Morris, included Rufus King (left) and his father-in-law Philip Schuyler (right).

James Monroe, Burr, Livingston, and others were now publicly attacking Washington as an "Angloman," a monarchist, and a traitor.

In July 1795, confidential documents seized aboard a captured French ship provided evidence that Jefferson's agent, Secretary of State Edmund Randolph, had agreed to take money from the French government in return for promoting a pro-French policy. When Washington confronted him with the evidence, Randolph did not deny it, but resigned on the spot. Then, in the summer of 1796, Washington dismissed Monroe—another Virginian and a Jeffersonian agent—as his Minister to France, when reports from Paris revealed that Monroe was holding secret meetings with French officials, conspiring to effect a military alliance between France and the United States. When Monroe returned to America, he published a lengthy defense of his ambassadorship and accused Washington of treason for dismissing him.[4]

Against All Odds

Alexander Hamilton was *always* in the minority. He was in the minority at Philadelphia in 1787. He was in the minority during the Washington Presidency. His power did not come from winning the majority of citizens to his views. He was never a "politician." He oper-

---

4. In 1794 Washington had nominated John Marshall to succeed Gouverneur Morris as Minister to France, but when Marshall declined, Washington, who was under pressure to appoint a Virginian, reluctantly named Monroe.

ated from a higher view of the battle, and at certain key, opportune moments he struck, with all of his intellectual prowess, to achieve breakthroughs which could then be built upon. Each attack, each breakthrough, then redefined new opportunities for what was possible. His power, his weapon, was his mind.

The election of John Adams in 1796, on the other hand, brought into the Presidency an individual who had no commitment to the vision of Hamilton's revolution. The *principles* and the *mission* which had guided the nation between 1789 and 1797 vanished from the office of the Presidency. Exacerbating the problem was Adams' deep personal hatred of Hamilton. He called Hamilton "debauched," a "creole," an "opium addict," that "bastard brat," and accused him of "cavorting with whores." He repeated Jefferson's slander that Hamilton was a monarchist and pro-British. Adams, never a man to be guided by discretion, uttered publicly much of the filth that he slung at Hamilton. Abigail Adams, if anything, despised Hamilton more than her husband and refused to wear black after he was murdered.

Under Adams' gross mis-leadership, the Federalist

Portrait by Samuel Morse
Jefferson agent James Monroe, shown here, was dismissed as Minister to France by George Washington.

John and Abigail Adams despised Hamilton, and Adams' presidency had no commitment to Hamilton's vision.

Party fractured and disintegrated. Individuals of inferior intellect and morality began to flake off, and others, driven by greed and ambition, engaged in foolish, even treasonous schemes. As for Jefferson and his friends, their treasonous onslaught did not change in character at all. It simply escalated.

'Tis that strategic reality which defines the true nature of the career of Aaron Burr. A founding member of the anti-Hamilton *"Delenda est Carthago"* clique in 1791, an organizer against the Jay Treaty in 1795, Burr headed the New York Tammany Society by 1797, the flagship Jeffersonian organization in New York City. Two years later he established the Manhattan Corporation as a financial base for his operations and as a means by which to pry Federalist Party leaders away from Hamilton through bribery. His assigned task was to destroy Hamilton's power base in New York, to leave Hamilton without means to continue the fight.

Cross-Party Treason

Following Aaron Burr's failed attempt to seize the Presidency from Thomas Jefferson in the election of 1800, and his recruitment of Federalist Party leaders to that effort, Burr embarked on a non-stop effort to split the Federalist Party and shatter Hamilton's political leadership in New York State.

Beginning in 1801, Burr began to strip away vulnerable Federalist leaders from their allegiance to Hamilton. On February 22, 1802 Burr attended a meeting of top Federalists in Washington, D.C., and then, in the summer of that year, he embarked on a tour of the South, meeting with and wooing Federalist leaders.

By 1804, the nominally Democratic-Republican Burr was back in New York and announcing his intention to run for state governor. Federalist Party leaders flocked to Burr's banner, and the unprincipled Burr fanned the flames of division and disunion with attacks on Jefferson's Louisiana Purchase. When Hamilton spoke out publicly, strongly supporting the addition of the Louisiana Territory to the Union, he was widely denounced by Federalist leaders for doing so.

Hamilton published an electoral broadside to the people of New York, titled *Lansing or Burr*, wherein he warned that Burr was conspiring with Northeast Federalists to dismember the Union. Hamilton endorsed Burr's opponent, the Democratic-Republican Lansing, and when Lansing withdrew from the race, Hamilton endorsed the new Democratic-Republican candidate Morgan Lewis. Lewis eventually won the election. Federalist-controlled newspapers, which had enthusiastically backed Burr, vilified Hamilton and ostracized him within the Federalist Party.

Earlier, in the spring of 1804, Timothy Pickering, now a Senator from Massachusetts, had conducted a tour of New York. His goal was to recruit leading local Federalists into a plan for the secession of New York and New England from the Union. Pickering and the so-called Essex Junto[5] called for the creation of a northern confederacy, "exempt from the corrupt and corrupting influence and oppression of the aristocratic Democrats of the South." Many New York Federalists were receptive to this message, but Hamilton told one associate, "You know there cannot be any political confidence between Mr. Jefferson and his administration and myself. But I view the suggestion of such a project with horror."

Hamilton placed the blame for these developments equally on the Essex Junto and on Jefferson. In a discussion with a friend, Adam Hoops, Hamilton stated that Jefferson's policies would result in "bloody anarchy," and he predicted, "The result must be destructive to the present Constitution and eventually the establishment of

---

5. The Essex Junto originated in Massachusetts as backers for ratification of the Constitution in 1788, and had been early supporters of the Washington Presidency. Its wealthy members, however, many of whom were involved in trade with British merchants, proved in the end to be far more loyal to wealth and power than to the Republic.

separate governments framed on principles in their nature hostile to civil liberty."

Four days before his death, in a conversation at his home in northern Manhattan, Hamilton said to John Trumbull, a New England Federalist, "You are going to Boston. You will see the principal men there. Tell them from Me, at My request, for God's sake, to cease these conversations and threatenings about a separation of the Union. It must hang together as long as it can be made to."

The Battle Engaged

During his nine years in New York City, from 1795 to 1804, Hamilton's position was one of a commander-in-chief in a theater of total war. His power was in his ideas, and his ideas were interventions, designed to enable a population to perceive the possibility of a better future, a better life, a greater potentiality. He authored articles, essays, speeches, resolutions, and letters. In one 68-day period, he wrote more than 100,000 words!— all of which were published in New York newspapers. Jefferson and Madison were terrified of him.

In 1801, Hamilton founded the *New York Post*, which would function as his political voice in New York City. In 1802, he wrote to Senator James Bayard,[6] proposing the creation of a new movement which Hamilton called the Christian Constitutional Society.[7] It was intended not merely to oppose the Jeffersonians, but to be the beginnings of an effort to effect a moral and cultural revival within the American people.

Charles Wilson Peale

Massachusetts Senator Timothy Pickering conspired with Aaron Burr for New England and New York to secede from the Union.

painted by Gilbert Stuart

Hamilton urged New England Federalist John Trumbull, shown here, to persuade his fellow Federalists in Boston to stop threatening the unity of the Union.

By 1804, consider where matters stood: Hamilton had succeeded completely in crushing Aaron Burr's power grab in New York State; he had declared war on the renegade elements within the Federalist Party; and he was preparing the groundwork to overturn Jefferson's counter-revolution. At the same time, Hamilton recognized that the greatest obstacle, the most serious difficulty to be addressed, was the post-1797 deterioration in the minds and morality of the American people, the degeneration of the nation's culture. This is reflected in a letter which Hamilton wrote to Gouverneur Morris, in which he states:

The time may ere long arrive when the minds of men will be prepared to make an effort to recover the Constitution, but the many cannot now be brought to make a stand for its preservation. We must wait a while.

This was not pessimism. It was an honest assessment of the battlefield. Singular historic opportunities are time specific. The poetic notion of *punctum saliens* is a rigorous scientific conception. Fighting the same battle over and over again with the same tactics will always fail, particularly if the conditions of the battlefield have changed. Yet, Hamilton was also developing new initiatives, new flanks to counterattack. He was redefining the battle as he went along. During this same period, Hamilton wrote another letter to Gouverneur Morris. In it he defines their common task:

But, my dear sir, we must not content ourselves with a temporary effort to oppose the approach of evil. We must derive instruction from the experience before us; and learning to form a just estimate of things to which we have been at-

---

6. In 1801, Bayard had followed Hamilton's advice and played a key role in the defeat of Burr. In 1802 he led the fight with Morris against the repeal of the Judiciary Act, and in 1812 he voted against Madison's declaration of war against Britain.

7. See Donald Phau, "Hamilton's Final Years: The Christian Constitutional Society," *EIR* Jan. 3, 1992.

tached, there must be a systematic and persevering endeavor to establish the fortune of a great empire on foundations much firmer than have yet been devised.

IV. 'Hamilton Must Die'

Hamilton was 47 years old when he died. He was younger than Jefferson, younger than Madison, only one year older than Monroe, and only ten years older than John Quincy Adams. He was closer in age to John Quincy Adams than he was to John Jay, who was twelve years his senior. Hamilton's career was not over. He was in his prime. It would certainly be an exaggeration to state that Hamilton was "just getting started," but he, most emphatically, was not finished.

In looking for the motives for Hamilton's murder, it would be a serious mistake to simply look at the details of his political activity. The danger he represented to the oligarchy was far more profound; it was of a type that all historians fail to grasp. In a letter to Madison, Thomas Jefferson had described Hamilton as an army, "a Host unto himself." Hamilton's very identity, and his willingness to risk all for principle, made him the most dangerous man in the world for the foreign and domestic enemies of the Republic.

Hamilton's intention was never merely to build factories or canals or bridges, but, rather, to unleash those slumbering powers within the minds and souls of the people of the nation, to effect a great cultural uplifting which would define new potentials for future victories, future advances, and a more human society.

A mind, a courageous personal-

Biographical Dictionary of the U.S. Congress
Hamilton proposed to Senator James Bayard (above) the launching of a moral and cultural revival within the American people.

ity, whose innermost identity embodies the principle of the creative flank, is the greatest danger imaginable to oligarchical rule. The actual motive for the murder of Hamilton was that *Hamilton's continued existence, alone, posed potential for the victory of his cause.*

The Death Squads

Much has been written about the Hamilton-Burr duel of 1804, but one glaring pattern is never mentioned. *Between 1795 and 1804, dueling was employed by the agents of both Thomas Jefferson and Aaron Burr as their primary method for carrying out a policy of assassination against Hamilton, his family, and other individuals deemed dangerous.*

In 1795, shortly after returning to New York City, Hamilton barely avoided a duel with James Nicholson, who called Hamilton an "abettor of Tories" and publicly accused him of having embezzled 100,000 pounds as Treasury Secretary. Nicholson was the President of the New York Democratic Society and a close friend of

James Nicholson (above), close friend of Jefferson and brother-in-law of Albert Gallatin, tried to engage Hamilton in a duel.

Jefferson. He was also the brother-in-law of Albert Gallatin. He played a key role in securing the vice-presidential nomination for Aaron Burr in 1800. This duel was prevented only through the last minute intervention of Rufus King and a young DeWitt Clinton.

In the summer of 1795, Hamilton was almost forced into another duel, this time with a man named Maturin Livingston, a Burr ally and member of the Tammany Society.

On May 21, 1798, William Keteltas, a Democratic-Republican lawyer who was close to both Jefferson and Burr, denounced Hamilton, threatening, "But like Caesar, you are ambitious and for that ambition to enslave his country, Brutus slew him. And are ambitious men less dangerous to American than

Roman liberty?" Replying in the same newspaper the next day, Hamilton declared, "By the allusion to Caesar and Brutus, he plainly hints at [my] assassination."

In 1799, Hamilton's brother-in-law, John Barker Church,[8] was challenged to a duel by Aaron Burr. Death was only avoided when, after the first volley of pistol shots failed to injure either man, Church apologized to Burr, and the duel was ended.

In November 20, 1801, Hamilton's eldest son, nineteen-year-old Philip, was challenged to a duel by George Eacker, a close ally of Aaron Burr. Philip was mortally wounded. He suffered for hours and died in the presence of his parents.

In 1802, another Burr agent, John Swartwout, forced DeWitt Clinton into a duel. Swartwout refused to end the duel after the first volley, and the duel continued for five volleys, only ending when Swartwout was unable to continue because he had been shot twice, in the hip and leg.

This murderous sequence of events culminated in Burr's murder of Hamilton in 1804. That story is well known. For weeks Hamilton did everything possible to prevent the duel, while Burr stalked him relentlessly. They exchanged numerous letters, and Hamilton bent over backward to satisfy Burr, but Burr would not be satisfied.

For the oligarchy, Hamilton had to die.

* * * *

Some say that Hamilton was rash and easily provoked, even that he brought death upon himself. Gouverneur Morris put it another way. In his eulogy over the dead body of Hamilton, Morris said,

> He disdained concealment. Knowing the purity of his heart, he bore it as it were in his hand, exposing to every passenger its inmost recesses. This generous indiscretion subjected him to cen-

Burr agent John Swartwout (above), forced Hamilton ally DeWitt Clinton into a duel in 1802.

sure from misrepresentation. His speculative opinions were treated as deliberate designs; and yet you all know how strenuous, how unremitting were his efforts to establish and to preserve the constitution.

In modern usage, one might say that Hamilton "wore his heart on his sleeve." He was not reckless; he was *fearless* in the defense of the Republic; *passionate* in the defense of his creation. He knew what he had created, and he knew what he had made possible for future generations, future human culture. That mission was his life. He could not be turned back or turned aside.

V. Future Flanks

At the May 14 LaRouche PAC Manhattan Dialogue with Lyndon LaRouche, the following exchange took place:

Question: So, if we look at what Putin is doing, what Hamilton did with his life ... how do we get people on a mass scale, within the United States, to think like these guys?

LaRouche: Well, you have to *be* like them. You have to be devoted to a mission like that which they had adopted. And people who are able to do that are in society generally, particularly in the United States, *very rare*. So you have to get out of all those categories, and do something and be something which is *very rare*. Achieve it, if you can.

Finally, we turn our attention to three initiatives which drew Hamilton's devotion in the last years of his life. He never stopped fighting, and he never stopped creating. New flanks by which to catch the enemy off guard, new initiatives intended to create new possibilities for victory—that was the nature of Hamilton's evolving repertoire. Be aware, however, that these were not simply limited "nice projects." In 1804, Jefferson was in the White House, and the Federalist Party was

---

8. In the 1780s, John Barker Church was one of the two principal shareholders in Robert Morris' Bank of North America, and later it was his capital which Hamilton used to establish the Bank of New York. His son, Philip Schuyler Church, later became a co-founder of the Erie Canal Company.

nonfunctional. Hamilton was initiating a series of new battles, new flanks, intended to create new potentialities for the purpose of overthrowing the evil that had taken control of the nation.

Slavery

In January of 1798, Hamilton resumed his association with the New York Manumission Society, his personal affiliation having lapsed during his service as Treasury Secretary. He was elected the Society's legal adviser, and he helped defend free blacks when out-of-state slave masters brandished bills of sale and tried to snatch them off the New York streets. In 1799, through the efforts of the society and Governor John Jay, the New York State Assembly decreed the gradual abolition of slavery in New York State by a vote of 68 to 23.

The Manumission Society also established and ran a school for one hundred black children, teaching them spelling, reading, writing, and arithmetic. Hamilton also, as the society's lawyer, brought suits in court to prevent New York slaveholders from selling their slaves to the South, whence they would be transferred to the West Indian sugar plantations. Hamilton maintained his role as the society's legal adviser until the day of his death.[9]

The Erie Canal

It was Hamilton's father-in-law, Philip Schuyler, who first began exploring the possibility of building canals and developing New York's upstate water system. He drafted a plan as early as 1776 and showed it to Charles Carroll and Benjamin Franklin. In 1792, with Elkanah Watson, he formulated a project for a canal between the Hudson River and Lake Ontario. Schuyler continued his efforts throughout his life, and in the summer of 1802, when 69 years old, he examined personally the entire western canal route, devising improvements for locks and solving the engineering and

The Park Street Theater was founded as a Classical theater by William Dunlap (above). Hamilton was legal adviser to the theater.

mathematical problems himself.

Then, in 1800, Gouverneur Morris drafted detailed plans for a canal to Lake Erie which he submitted to the New York Surveyor General. In 1801 Morris toured the entire region, exploring the topology and the obstacles to a future canal. Morris worked intensely on this project, eventually succeeding in getting the New York State legislature, in 1810, to establish the Erie Canal Commission, with Morris, Steven Van Rensselaer, and DeWitt Clinton as its leaders.

Hamilton is usually not associated with the Erie Canal, but the topic is raised here for two reasons. First, to make the point that the entire project originated with, and was led by, Hamilton's relatives and his closest friends; second, to recognize that the creation of the canal involved the best elements of both the Federalist and Democratic-Republican parties. It was a bipartisan effort, and its success gives some indication of the potential flank, had Hamilton lived, for the ultimate defeat of the Virginia slavocracy.

The Park Theater[10]

The Park Street Theater was founded in Manhattan in 1798, by William Dunlap. It grew out of earlier efforts by Dunlap to bring classical theater to New York. On opening night, Shakespeare's *As You Like It* was the first performance to be staged.

Hamilton was the legal adviser to the theater, and Dunlap consulted Hamilton on disputes surrounding the theater's financing. Dunlap was himself an active member of the Manumission Society, a leading advocate of eliminating slavery, and a trustee of the Free School for African Children.

One hundred subscribers put up the funds for the theater. Among them were Hamilton's friend Stephen Van Rensselaer; James Watson, Rensselaer's running mate in the 1800 gubernatorial race; William Bayard, a close friend of Hamilton, and the man at whose home he died in 1804; DeWitt Clinton, the individual most

---

9. In 1785, Hamilton, Jay, Morris, and Van Rensselaer had all been founding members of the New York Manumission Society, with Jay as the first president. Earlier, Morris had authored the first proposal for abolition of slavery in New York State in 1778.

---

10. Material for this section was provided through the labors of Renee Sigerson.

responsible for the building of the Erie Canal; Nathaniel Fish, named by Hamilton as the executor of his will; and Rufus King, who, next to Morris, was Hamilton's closest political ally.

In 1825, it would be at the Park Theater that the first opera to be performed in Italian in New York City, Rossini's *The Barber of Seville*, was staged. An Italian opera troupe was imported for the occasion.

* * * *

Hamilton's life calls out to us today from across the centuries. It is a compelling echo, a light, a living voice. At Hamilton's funeral, Gouverneur Morris posed a question, a yardstick by which we might examine our own decisions, our own motivations. Morris asked, "What would Hamilton do?" Properly understood, that is a good question. But a simple reading of that question falls short. The personal issue before each of us requires more than simply attempting to lead a good life, attempting to do what is right. It requires more even than raw courage. It most certainly requires more than simply parroting support for the right "issues" or the "correct program."

Between 1781 and 1797, Hamilton brought into ex-

istence a new reality, a new potential for future human development. Everything that was made possible by that creation, existed within a universe created by Hamilton, a universe which flowed from new principles, alien to the oligarchical forces which surrounded it. And, although those forces were determined to destroy it, Hamilton's Victory created a breathing space, a period of time, in which a new future existence for humanity was made manifest.

Is our situation any different today? Are we capable of creating that new universe? Are we willing to undergo the agony required to bring such a creation into existence? What are the consequences if we fail? As Lyndon LaRouche has said, *"The only way you can ever win is by doing something which has never been done before in human history."* What does this imply as to one's own identity? What new powers must we summon from within ourselves to "do something that has never been done before"? Do not admire Hamilton. Examine what he did, how he fought, how his mind worked—and act accordingly.

Special thanks to Lyndon LaRouche and Tony Papert for their cooperation in bringing this article to its final form.

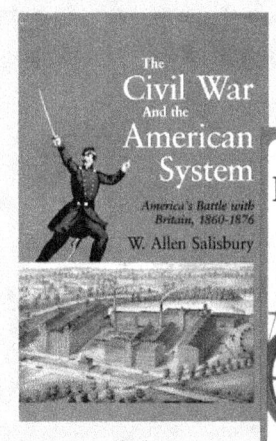
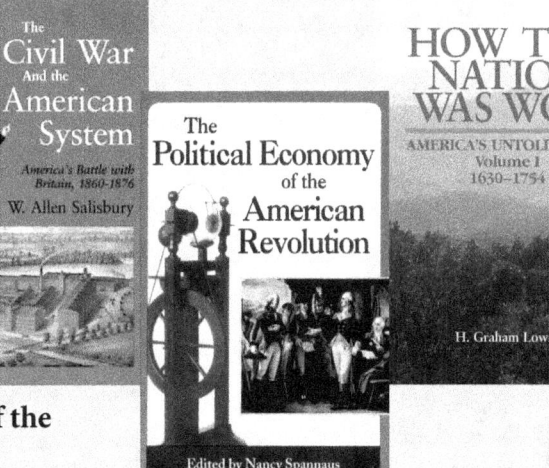

www.ingramcontent.com/pod-product-compliance
Lightning Source LLC
Chambersburg PA
CBHW081156280526
45787CB00008B/3346